RIVER
OF
MYSTERY

DAN BOMKAMP
J.L. FREDRICK
RON NAGEL

First Edition

ISBN: 0615961193
ISBN-13: 978-0615961194

Printed in the United States of America

Cover design by Lovstad Publishing
Copyedit by Joel Lovstad
Cover photo, Wisconsin River by Ron Nagel

ACKNOWLEDGMENTS

Joseph E. Kapler, Curator, Wisconsin Historical Society for his enthusiasm, insight, and guidance; Andy Kraushaar, Visual Material Curator, WHS, for his extensive research support; Andy Cockroft, great-great grandson of Paul Seiftert, for his numerous family files and pictures; Jutta Wiese, Archivist, Dresden University of Technology, Germany, for extensive research and providing critical information and pictures of Paul Seifert's early life and family; Petra Hesse, University of Leipez, Germany, for providing information about Paul Seifert's education background; Kevin Kurdylo & Antje Petty, Max Kade Institue for German-American Studies, for background information and moral support; Len Larsandro, Paper Conservator, Madison, Wisconsin, one of few people capable of identifying a Seifert painting; Paula Holahan, Curator of Mammals & Birds, for her efforts to identify Paul Seifert's taxidermy work; Crystal Foley, Richland County History Room, Richland Center, Wisconsin, for providing Richland County history; Richard Slaughter, Director of Dept. of Geoscience, UW, Madison, for quality information; James Hibbard, Archivist, UW, Platteville, for his diligent research; James Schneider, local historian; Lee Harris, Lost Treasure Magazine publisher; Steven Huxmann, German translation services; Dennis Daggett, archival services; Patti Newball, part owner of Bogus Bluff LLC; Gary Soule, Wisconsin Speleological Society historian.

The Archaeological Resources Protection Act of 1979, also referred to as ARPA, is a federal law of the United States passed in 1979 and amended in 1988. It governs the excavation of archaeological sites on federal and Indian lands in the United States, and the removal and disposition of archaeological collections from those sites.

More information can be found online:
http://www.nps.gov/archeology/tools/Laws/arpa.htm

CONTENTS

Introduction   vii

Fact, Fiction, and the Unknown   11

Caves and Glaciers   26

The Driftless Area   30

Glacial Lake Wisconsin   33

The River   35

Early People   37

Caves—Archeological Storehouses   55

Bogus Bluff   58

A Treasure in Gold   67

The Pine River Delta   71

Richland City   75

Gotham   89

The Young Paul Seifert   95

Paul Comes to Richland City   99

Real or Hoax?   107

Paul Seifert the Painter   111

Richland City Today   119

A Place of Enchantment   121

References and Sources   123

About the Authors   126

INTRODUCTION

Inquisitive nineteen-year old Ron Nagel read an article in a magazine titled *Indian Treasure Cave* in 1978. The story stirred his interest; he made his first trip to the hills between Gotham and Muscoda, Wisconsin looking for the cave cited in the story, and to this day, he has not given up. Subsequently, a 35-year-long search and countless hours of research on this and related topics have inspired the creation of this book. Following is the intriguing magazine story that started it all:

Indian Burial Cave

By E. Scott Colvin

From *Lost Treasure Magazine,* June 1978

When Paul A Seifert emigrated from his native Austria* to the United States, he brought with him a love of adventure and exploration. Settling on the banks of the Wisconsin River in Gotham, Wisconsin, he became immediately enchanted with the picturesque river bluffs.

One day while exploring the bluffs near the "lost" village of Richland City at the mouth of the Pine River, Sei-

fert located the opening of a cave. With difficulty he worked his way through the narrow passageway and found himself in a chamber filled with jewelry, ancient pottery vessels, stone and copper implements, bones of extinct animals, and Indian skeletons.

Excited by his find, Seifert wrote to an archeologist friend in Austria by the name of Von Wolfgang and also sent him a few of the Indian relics. Von Wolfgang then made a trip to Richland City and upon his return home published an account of his visit in a Vienna newspaper. Seifert would not permit his friend to remove any of the buried treasures and to be certain that no one else would remove the cave's contents he sealed the entrance by blasting the rock.

Seifert died some years ago and in the intervening years treasure hunters from Richland Center, Watertown, Monroe, Wyocena and other nearby towns have tried to locate the cave. In so far as it is known, all attempts have been unsuccessful and the contents of Seifert's treasure cave still await some lucky treasure hunter.

*Paul Seifert was actually from Germany.

RIVER
OF
MYSTERY

Fact, Fiction, and the Unknown

Legends are created with three main ingredients: a bit of truth, a bit of fiction, and a generous portion of the unknown. At the core of this book's topic is a legend that has all that and more; it comes from the land untouched by the Ice Age glaciers—a place in North America continually inhabited by humans for the last six thousand years. Pre-historic man slowly gave way to the Native American culture that, in turn, gave way to an influx of European settlers. Among them, a German emigrant named Paul Seifert eventually made his home here. He and all those before him have contributed to keeping the legend alive.

Located somewhere in Richland County, Wisconsin is Big Eagle Cave, not to be confused with the popular tourist cave that shares a similar name—*Eagle Cave*, located about ten miles southwest of Richland Center. (*Eagle Cave* was first discovered in early Twentieth Century by a man said to be tracking a bear, leading him into a hole in the ground that turned out to be an enormous onyx cave.) *Big Eagle Cave* is the subject of a Native American legend that has been passed through the ages by the Winnebago Indians of Wisconsin. In 1938 the Wisconsin Historical Society recorded their best understanding of this story to preserve it for future generations.

From *WISCONSIN ARCHEOLOGIST*
Vol. 18, No. 2, April 1919, Victor S. Craim

Around Big Eagle Cave, Richland County, the fabric of mystery has been woven by Indian legend. Here, even today, baffling mysteries confront the experienced explorer and adventurer. They concern the numerous caves that honeycomb the region covering a large portion of Richland County. Most of these are small, yet some are hundreds of feet long with ceilings far above one's head, and some, like the Big Eagle Cave, are filled with beautiful calcite deposits, presenting a marvelous display of stalactites, and stalagmites.

According to Big Eagle Cave legend, the entire populace of the Winnebago village was lost in its mysterious labyrinths, and their skeletons and artifacts lay strewn over the floor, yet it is questionable whether any white man has ventured into these challenging realms to learn the culture of this vanished tribe. One can only question the reality, yet, a survey of the region, would lead one to believe that there is some truth in the legend.

In the far, dim past of this tribe, so long ago that the exact time has been lost to memory, three Indian youths left this village one day to hunt deer in the hills. When they failed to return for two days, Great Eagle, the chief of the tribe, sent a band of warriors to follow their trail, fearing that the three boys may have been captured by hostile Sacs and taken prisoner. The trail led to the head of a deep ravine and ended at the mouth of a cave, into which the trail entered but from which it failed to emerge. Two or three braves made rude torches and entered the yawning black cavern, leaving the others without. When they also failed to return, and the evening sun was fast sinking, the braves outside impatiently called down to them, but received no answering shout. As the callers strained to listen, they were perplexed and amazed to hear, very faintly, as though it came from the ends of the earth, the "Death Song" of an Indian. It was weirdly beautiful, far beyond anything they had ever heard. So incongruous a thing startled them and very soon, as it continued, their perplexity grew into uneasiness. What could it mean? Of the remaining eight, six grasped their weapons and darted into the cave. They, too, did not return. But the sun was all but gone in the west and to the straining ears of the waiting pair came only the faint and strangely magnificent "Song of the Indian's Death." Their uneasiness increased; by the time the evening shadows were creeping into the ravine, it had ripened into an unearthly fear. Back they hurried to the camp of Great Eagle, with an ever-increasing terror in their breasts.

Next day Great Eagle himself led 100 braves to the cave. The main body stayed without, while thirty warriors and five torch bearers cautiously slid into the great black hole. Very soon their lights had disappeared, as did all sound of them, and to the call of those without came answering echoes and the plaintive notes of the "Song of Death."

In desperation Great Eagle formed his men in a human chain, hand clutching hand. The first man led them courageously into the cavern. He had gone but a short distance when the second man suddenly realized that his hand, which but a moment before had held that of the leader, was clutching nothing! Quickly he reached forward, but as quickly the hand of the third man lost the hand of the second. There had not been a sound of a fall or of any violence. In terror the remaining human chain drew back out of the cave. Great Eagle held a council.

Perhaps what a hand could not hold a stout rope could, Great Eagle reasoned, as he tied the end of a stout rope most securely around the waist of a volunteer. He was to jerk the rope as he proceeded in, and to be pulled out by the men on the outside as soon as his jerking ceased. In he went. He had not gone far when his jerks on the rope ceased. As quickly as lightning the men hauled in the rope. But there came out of the cave only an empty loop, tied just as it had been when put around the man. The man had vanished. There was not a mark on the rope. A ghostly terror settled upon the people in the ravine, the stark silence broken again by the strains of the "Song of Death."

Great Eagle forbade anyone going near the cave, an edict needing no enforcing, except for the foolhardy few, led by too curious a spirit, who dared to investigate, never to return.

Now, after many moons there came from the forest a man, the like of whom had never been seen before. His skin was pale and soft, his hair white and silken; a great white beard reached to his waist. He was blind and understood not the tongue of the Winnebago, nor was he understood by them. He was led by an Indian boy of ten summers, with a longing, far-away look in his eyes, too old for his years. This Indian boy looked like one of those who had first gone into the cave even "the mother claimed him for her own but the boy maintained that he came from a tribe far to the northwest. This boy also served as the old man's interpreter.

It was soon evident that this strange man with long beard was a great healer with powers far beyond those of any local medicine man. In a comparatively short time, because of his unusual skill, power, and kindness, he was called "The Great Healer" by the Winnebago, and was revered by everyone.

One day Great Eagle told the Great Healer, through the boy, his interpreter, of the Indian "Song of Death."

"Lead me to this cave," said the blind healer.

And Great Eagle led him to the ravine, all the people following and forming a great semi-circle about the mouth of the cave. Not a sound disturbed the forest as all eyes watched the Great Healer and his youthful guide walk slowly and deliberately down in the darkness. Again there came the "Song of Death," but louder now and closer it seemed, so that the leaves of the trees stirred to and fro to its rhythm. All the warriors in the assembly nervously fingered their weapons.

The footsteps of the two going into the cave finally died out and, with a suddenness that filled the ravine with an alarming silence, the "Song of Death" *stopped. Then, faintly at first, but gradually louder, the sound of footsteps came from the cave, until after an endless waiting, the lone figure of the Great Healer issued from the cave. His eyes were closed and a beautiful, calm and serene smile delicately touched his lips. He stopped, lifted his face and arms toward the sun, whose slanting evening rays filtered down through the leaves, and in an unknown tongue he sang the "Song of Death" while he walked slowly and deliberately toward the river, the people following. At the river's edge he stepped into a canoe, and without a paddle the canoe swung into the river, carrying the Great Healer away no one knew where.*

Several days later, a brave, bolder than his companions, ventured into the silent cave. To the amazement of his comrades, who had tried to prevent his entrance, he came out again saying that he had followed the cavern until it became so low that he would have been forced to crawl had he gone farther.

With another companion he again entered and this time the two crawled on hands and knees until they reached a gigantic room. After lighting a torch their light revealed the skeletons of hundreds of Indians, lying face downward with arms outstretched toward a gigantic throne formed in the far wall. The great throne was empty. In terror the two Indians returned to the outer light and told their story.

Great Eagle and his council surmised that the cave was sacred to some great spirit, and decreed that the cavern entrance be closed with dirt and rocks. After a few generations even the story of the cave was lost, save by a certain few story-loving warriors of the forest.

It is not difficult to determine that there is ample fiction contained within this story; it may have been infused simply by the natural process of repeated story telling from generation to generation, each rendition gaining mass and momentum. But could there be a bit of truth? That is harder to ascertain. To understand if the possibility of such a cave exists, examination of regional geology and history is necessary.

Also at the core of this book's topic is another tale that could possibly support the element of truth in the Winnebago Indian legend. Fortunately, this story is more recent in origin, and facts are more easily sorted from the fiction. Originally composed in German, its translation can be excused from some awkward English. Segments of this tale of *The Rose Colored Spear* will be further discussed later in the book as the mystery unfolds.

"Here in my studio in Vienna, Austria, having re-turned last week from a trip to Wisconsin, U.S. of America. Before me on my desk, lies a spear of Wisconsin quartzite of ancient American workmanship. It is a splendid specimen, 13 inches long, three and one half inches wide in the middle. On that specimen hangs a tale I will try to give the reader. Before I commence my story I will say something about myself, and the principal actors in this tale.

I the son of an Austrian Nobleman was sent to the University of Leipzig, Saxon, Germany to study philosophy, to follow the custom of all the young men of my station. Arrived in the spring of the year 1865 at night. I met the next morning after my arrival on the old campus of the University two brothers – sons of a Saxon Aristocrat. We got acquainted, soon we were friends, roommates, and at last we loved each other like brothers. It was a vast difference in the character of the two brothers. Joseph the oldest was a noble, high minded young man. A thinker, philosopher, a perfect gentleman. Paul, the younger, a regular fellow. Always hard up in spite of his father's generous allowance, always in mischief, generous to a fault. True, and friend to me. So we lived an ideal student life for two semesters. In the early spring of the year of 1866 rumors of war commence circulating thru the old University town. Very soon the dogs of war commence howling. Soon we were called to our regiments. I to Linz, Austria, the two brothers to Dresden, Saxony to join their regiments. In the evening of the second day of July 1866 we met again in the camp before Sadowa, Austria, knowing the next day will bring on a great battle. A foreboding of evil hanging over us. Joseph always sedate told us whatever will be our fate the next day to do our duty to God and our Country, and if it is the Lord's will, so that we have to enter the other life, we went there not ashamed to meet our dear once gone before. Paul's answer was "I hope the Good Lord will then provide a few gallons of nectar to soften our black bread." This remark showed the difference of character of the two brothers. At evening of the next day I was wounded and carried from the battlefield. Joseph fell under the terrible charge of the Prussian guards, and Paul was taken to the Prussian Fortress of Stralsund, a prisoner, as I was informed after. Now I will commence the Tale of the rose colored Spearhead.

In the Spring of 1887 one morning I received, like always, my mail from the postman. Amongst my letters was one post stamp Richland City, Wisconsin North America. Judge my surprise, who could know me in that far of Country? I opened the letter, it was from Paul. He wrote that he had escaped from Stralsund, went on board of an American ship, landed at New York, drifted to northern Wisconsin, came down the Wisconsin river on a raft, got acquainted with a German Patriot living at Richland City, married his daughter, a beautiful girl of 17, lived happy, had 4 girls, and still had his old disease hanging over him. The consumption of the Pocket Book. So we renewed our friendship by letter. I am an archeologist. My hope; to collect relics from different Country. I have asked Paul once in my letters to him if he could find and send me some relics of the American Aboriginies. In a very short period of time, I received a package thru a New York transfer house. It contained the most magnificent relics of American prehistoric times. Great ancient copper spears, arrow and spears of different colors of quartzite, great flint spears of different and very rare forms, 2 great spears of obsidian, butterfly ceremonials, birdstones, celt of flint, a breastplate of ancient copper, battle-axes, celts, and more. So he has sent me package af-

ter package at different times til I had a collection of American ancient relics the imperial Museum at Vienna, Austria could not duplicate. Knowing that his financial circumstances would not allow him to purchase those priceless relics I wrote to him, not to sacrifice his and the welfare of his family, on my account. He wrote back to me "Those relics cost me nothing more than a little work and a few cold chills across my back. If you ever will make me a visit I will show you the place where I find those relics." Not understanding his remarks I dropped the subject. So the years passed. We kept exchanging letters, receiving more valuable relics at different times.

In the year 1901 I received a letter from Paul's wife. She wrote "If you want to see Paul once more, come soon. His old enemy Whiskey has the better of him; he cannot [last] a half year longer." After receiving that letter I packed my suitcase and started for Gotham. Taking passage on a Hamburg liner, I landed at New York alright. Took the Western train and arrived at Gotham, Wisconsin sound and well. Having telegraphed from New York to Paul he met me at the depot in Gotham. I found Paul looking better than I expected to find him, after the remark in his wife's letter. He had, with God's his Glorious Redeemers help, quit the Whiskey habit, and has started on a different life to repay his faithful wife for her sacrifice in the past dark days of selfishness.

We had happy days together hunting, fishing, visiting the ancient village sites around Richland City, living in the old memories of the past. Paul and family lived in a long low cottage on the banks of the old Wisconsin River, amongst his flowers, one ideal home, his wife a perfect lady and his two daughters at home, the oldest girls being married.

So came the last night of my visit. Tomorrow I must start for home. It was a beautiful moonlit night. I spoke to Paul about his promise to show me the place where he has found the relics. He said, "Will you follow me where I lead?" My reply was, "I shall be your shadow." His wife was very concerned. "Don't endanger your friend and yourself." "We will be back for breakfast little wife, don't worry."

His boat he kept in the shadow of a magnificent large maple tree below his house. He put some ropes, a bull's eye lantern and some torches in the boat. One of the ropes had a large iron hook on one end. I stepped in the boat. He took the oars and we floated down the beautiful river till we reached the foot of the old historic Bogus Bluff. Here he hooked the boat to the roots of an old cottonwood tree. Then we climbed to the summit of old Bogus. What a beautiful sight met our eyes. Across the gleaming shadows of the river under the protecting shadows of the southern bluffs little Avoca sleeps. Secure downstream among the dark green of the forest flash the lights of Muscoda and miles the other direction on the north river bank Lone Rock shows dimly, and from the gloom of the river burst in accents heard the call of the Great Horned Owl; shadow and voice of the forest.

"Let us go," Paul said, "Time flies."

We passed from ridge to ridge. Sometimes through large timber, sometimes through under-brush, until we, the best I could guess, had traveled about two miles. At last we stopped on a ridge here and there covered by great fragments of rock in front of a large ledge. Here Paul unloosened the rope he'd brought with him with a large hook and threw the hook over the roots of a large cedar about ten feet above us. He climbed and told me to follow. We landed on a very narrow ledge. Before us was a very narrow crevice hardly wide to let us in. Inside the crevice a black hole lay before us. Paul lit his lantern and commenced to go down that black pas-sage way and told me to follow. We went down, down in the mountain, how far I could not tell. Sometimes we fell, sometimes we slid until at last we reached the sand bottom of a great cave. Frag-ments of rock were everywhere and amongst those were great bones of prehistoric animals. Here and there also were the antlers of deer and elk.

We left that cave and I followed Paul along pas-sageways looking like the dry beds of an under-ground river. At last we stood at an abyss black and dangerous looking. Paul fastened the end of a large rope around a projecting rock and went down the rope. I followed. We went down about 35 or 40 feet and landed in just about such a passageway like the one above until we reached another cave. Here Paul lit one of the torches he carried.

What a beautiful sight. A light reflecting from

pendant stalactites with which the ceiling was covered forming a miniature imitation of a starlit heaven. Paul would not stop here long. We went through long passages winding through the mountain until these got so small that we had sometimes to creep on hand and feet. At last we reached another cave.

Dark and damp air surrounded us. Here Paul lit another torch. Friends, I cannot describe the horror I felt. The bottom of the cave was covered with skeletons of a vanished race. Skulls were everywhere. Here perished a tribe, very near I should say, a nation. Their belongings scattered amongst the bones. Battle axes of stone, ancient pottery, whole and in fragments, flint arrows and spears, whole and broken everywhere. Here Paul said, "Here is the mine of the relics I have sent you."

Now I understood his remark, "work and chills down his back." How true. And in this horrible place he went many times to please me.

Here on a shelf of stone I found that beautiful rose quartzite spear beside the bones of a human hand. I described it in the opening chapter of this tale. So we went along the cave 'till we entered another passage, beginning to hear a curious noise. As we went further it sounded louder, more and more so 'till it sounded like the howling of a lot of maniacs and the moaning of the dying under torture. I ask Paul to tell me, for the love of heaven to tell me what is that terrible noise? "Falling waters and the rushing of the wind through the crevices above." All at once I saw a blue light flicker here and there. It came nearer and nearer. Paul's answer: nothing more __ dampness and __ could stand any more. (two words were un-decipherable) Oh how horrible. "Oh Paul, let us go and get out of here." So we retraced our steps through the cave of the dead. We stopped before the skeleton of a woman. Around her fleshless neck she had a necklace of matchless beauty composed of quartzite disks of different colors held together by bands of ancient copper. I wanted to take it. Paul said, "It is put there by the hand of love. Her spirits would mourn if you take it." We passed on and made our way back to the long rope. Climbed up, and passed through cave and passage 'till we stood on the ledge, ready to descend to the ground and to our way home the same way as we came to our boat. Found it alright. We rowed up the river. Day was breaking as we landed at Paul's home. His wife welcomed us. Breakfast was ready. After that Paul escorted me to the depot of Gotham and the train started.

"Good bye Paul." "Adios Sebe Wofl." "Till we meet again across the great divide."

Arrived home after eventless voyage and never will forget as long as I live that terrible journey to the Caves of the Dead, under the Bluff of the old Wisconsin. S.v.W."

Translated from the German by P.A.S.

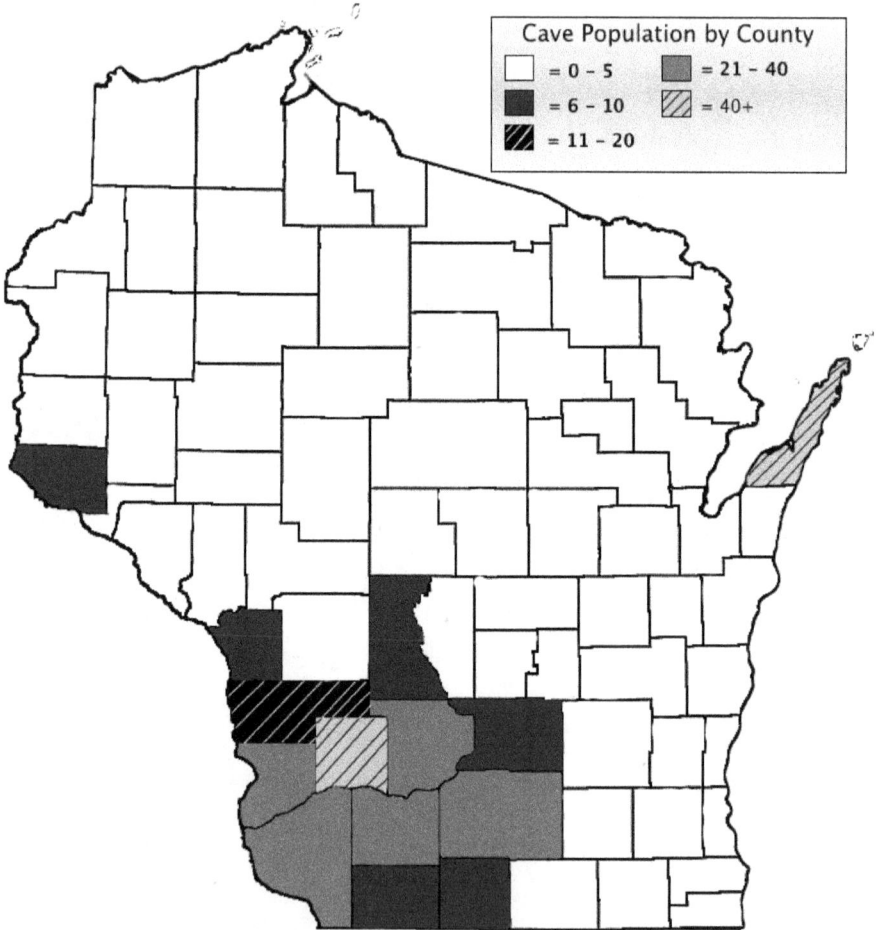

Highest concentration of caves found in southwestern
counties of Wisconsin. (Graphic by Jake Nagel)

Caves and Glaciers

To effectively tell the story of Paul Seifert, Bogus Bluff and Richland City we must first go back to the time when the Lower Wisconsin River Valley was first formed by glaciers that advanced and receded over a period of two million years.

Not all of Wisconsin is rich in caves. The seven counties that make up southwestern Wisconsin have the highest concentration with 210 of the total 274 known caves in the entire state. Crawford County has 27; Dane County, 32; Grant County, 33; Iowa County, 33; Richland County, 41; Sauk County, 27; and Vernon County, 17.

Why are there only 64 caves in the rest of the state? (Of these 64 caves, 34 of them are found in the Door County peninsula.) There is a reasonable and logical explanation that can be summed up in one word: *glaciers*.

Wisconsin has been glaciated four times in the last two million years. Glaciers are often thought of as huge ice sheets, a thousand feet to a mile thick and thousands of miles wide grinding across the landscape like a huge bulldozer. But this is not the case. Glaciers flow slowly across the land and follow the shape of existing valleys and depressions in the land. In fact, the front face of a glacier has lobes, extending into these valleys, following the shape of the earth before them. Think of a baseball glove lying flat on a table and look at the fingers of the glove. That is what a glacier looks like as it flows across the land.

When we talk about a glacier flowing, we are talking about the movement of a few feet or inches in a year, a few yards in a century, or a few miles in a thousand years. It happens very slowly, and as the immense weight of the ice presses down on the earth, it grinds everything into sand, rocks and pebbles. The larger hard boulders such as granite are pushed along and rounded into smooth shapes. This material is called *glacial drift*.

To illustrate just how immense these ice sheets were, one has only to look at the Great Lakes. The lakes were created by the glaciers and filled with their melt water. Lake Superior, the deepest, was created when an immense glacier followed a depression in the earth's crust and filled the existing valley. The weight was so immense that the crust of the earth actually split apart causing a "rift valley"—the deepest part of Lake Superior at 1,335 feet.

Today there is concern that the Great Lakes are getting shallower because of overuse and drought. But in reality, when the glaciers passed over the area, the land was depressed by the massive weight and is now still "springing back" to where it was before the time of the glaciers. The last glacier melted only 10,000 years ago, just a blip in the history of the earth. Of course, there could be overuse, but much of the lower water level is due to the land becoming higher, making the water *appear* lower.

Each time Wisconsin was glaciated, glacial drift was pushed along and filled in depressions, valleys, and caves that existed at the time. Tons of boulders, rock and gravel filled the caves, erasing them from existence and sealing them forever. During each ice age the climate warmed; over thousands of years the glaciers melted, the ice disappeared and the landscape recovered with its new shape.

Then the climate cooled again; about 20,000 years ago the last glacier advanced relentlessly across Wisconsin, pushing and grinding its way southward. The Green Bay Lobe of this massive ice sheet advanced into the eastern part of the Baraboo Hills, sometimes called the Baraboo Range. There it dammed the ancient upper Wisconsin River and created a broad, flat sand plain known as Glacial Lake Wisconsin. The central portion of the state became the floor of a huge glacial lake that was about the size of the present day Great Salt Lake in Utah.

Driftless Area

The Driftless Area

The Wisconsin River valley is a part of a unique region in the country called the *Driftless Area*. This means that an area of about 15,000 square miles including southwestern Wisconsin, southeastern Minnesota and northeastern Iowa were never glaciated. This area has no "drift" or glacial debris. All of the rest of Wisconsin, Minnesota and most of Iowa and Illinois were scraped flat by four great ice age glaciers, but the *Driftless Area* somehow managed to escape the ice.

Scientists have concluded that each time one of the four glaciers advanced, they stopped just short of this special place. Natural valleys and ridges turned the ice aside each time, and by sheer luck, the area was left as it had always been. By studying the age of the drift deposited all around the *Driftless Area,* scientists have been able to date the material to the four ice ages, the last ending around 12,000 years ago. Consequently the area is an example of what the Midwest looked like before the ice ages.

The steep hills and deep valleys are still much like they were two million years ago. Some vegetation dates back to those pre-historic times. And, this is why there are hundreds of caves still intact. While almost all of the other caves in Wisconsin were filled with glacial debris—or drift—and were lost forever, the caves in the southwest remain the same as they were in ancient times.

But wait a minute! Door County has 34 caves. Why are those caves still there? Door County is *not* in the Driftless Area. The reason is that most Door County caves are not Solutional Caves like the ones found in the Driftless Area. The Door County caves are Sea Caves or Littoral Caves, formed primarily by wave action. Door County is surrounded by water; the cliffs and rock walls bordering Lake Michigan have been pounded by wave action for thousands of years. Water slamming into veins of limestone and other soft stone over and over has created caves that line the coast. They are different than the Solutional Caves of the Driftless Area and are much younger.

So, at the end of the last ice age, the Wisconsin River Valley remained much the same as it had been for several million years. But another event was quickly approaching that would change it and shape it to what we see there today.

Glacial Lake Wisconsin

As the climate warmed around 15,000 years ago, the Green Bay Lobe of the last glacier had created a dam at the eastern part of the Baraboo Range resulting in a lake that covered most of central Wisconsin. Vast amounts of water built up behind the ice dam and pressure increased on the natural dam. The warmer climate caused the Green Bay Lobe to recede and the dam failed. Billions of gallons of water drained rapidly around the east end of the Baraboo Range and flooded the ancient lower Wisconsin River valley.

The force of the water sliced through sandstone to the bedrock forming the Dells of Wisconsin. It continued down the broad river valley sweeping huge boulders and icebergs many miles downstream. The wide river valley had been eroded over millions years, but the huge volumes of glacial melt water released by the sudden emptying of Glacial Lake Wisconsin changed the shape and scope of the land.

Enormous amounts of sand and gravel carried by the rushing water acted much like a file that undercut the sandstone and dolomite shoreline rocks along the river. This torrent of abrasive water formed the faces of the steep bluffs into sheer

rock walls. The signs of the water eroding the hills and shoreline are visible all up and down the river valley. Many bluffs
overlooking the river—including Bogus Bluff—have bare rock
faces most likely caused by millions of gallons of water wash-
ing away much of the dirt at the base of the hills, causing a
landslides that left the rock exposed. Looking at water erosion
marks high on a river bluffs makes one wonder what it must
have looked like then, when the entire valley was a giant
churning river from one side to the other. It must have been an
amazing sight.

To give some perspective on the flood, we can look back to
June 9, 2008. On that day an earthen dam in the village of Lake
Delton failed. The two hundred sixty-seven acre lake drained
through the failed section of the dam, creating a four hundred
foot wide channel as it flowed to the Wisconsin River. The water destroyed homes and washed out highways and lakeside
structures. It took two hours to drain the lake completely.
Glacial Lake Wisconsin was 4,000 times larger than Lake Delton.

The River

The Wisconsin River is the longest river in the state—430 miles beginning at the Wisconsin/Michigan border area called *Lac Vieux Desert.* It meets the Mississippi River at Wyalusing and drains the entire central portion of the State of Wisconsin.

The first known white explorers to record information about the Wisconsin River by name were Father Jacques Marquette and Louis Jolliet in 1673. (Others had seen it earlier—Groseilliers and Radisson in 1654, and Father Claude Allouez in 1669, but they did not refer to it by any name.) Marquette wrote:

> *"We knew that, at three leagues from Maskoutens, was a River which discharged into Missisipi... The river on which we embarked is called Meskousing. It is very wide; it has a sandy bottom, which forms various shoals that render its navigation very difficult. It is full o islands Covered with Vines."*

During the early times of exploration, the phonetics and spelling of the name varied with each cartographer in passing years. Marquette spelled it "Meskousing" as the name was probably conveyed verbally to him by the Indians. Jean Baptiste Franquelin's map of 1688 shows "Ouisconsin," reflecting some French influence, and numerous variations followed. But that spelling seemed to be the most accepted; in 1780 John Long spoke of "Ouisconsin, a fine river," and Northwest territorial governor Winthrop Sargent in 1796 wrote the name "Ouisconsing." Zebulon Pike repeated Long's spelling in 1805, and Stephen Long's map charted in 1822 was the first time "Wisconsin" appeared. That spelling was declared the standard and was made legal by the territorial legislature in 1845.

All researchers and historians agree that the name is aboriginal, but its meaning has been disputed over the years. A British army officer traveling in the American West wrote in 1838: "This river has been very appropriately named by the Indians "the Stream of the Thousand Isles..." It was not stated which tribe so named it, but it is not consistent with the vocabularies of the Siouan-speaking Winnebago or the Algonquian-speaking Ojibwa, Sauk, Fox, Kickapoo, Potawatomi, or Menominee.

A missionary among the Chippewa wrote in 1891 that he learned the name to mean "muskrat house." This translation was confirmed in later years by another missionary to the Chippewa. Since then, many explanations have been considered: "wild, rushing channel" or "the gathering of waters" both seem appropriate, but are adamantly rejected by those knowledgeable of the Algonquian tongue. Countless translations in over 300 years are still inconclusive, and the true origin and meaning may never be known for sure.

Early People

Near the end of the Pleistocene Ice Age, a huge volume of the world's water was locked up in the monumental glaciers that covered most of the northern hemisphere. Sea levels 20,000 to 25,000 years ago were about 300 feet lower than they are currently.

When the sea levels dropped, a land bridge was exposed between Siberia and what is now Alaska. The land bridge is now named the Bering Land Bridge after the Danish explorer Vitus Bering who sailed into the area in 1728. This land bridge allowed people and animals to travel back and forth from Asia to North America until about 11,000 years ago when the climate warmed and the glaciers began to melt.

Archeological evidence shows that these people traveled along the Pacific coast, as the climate along the ocean was warmer and free of ice. Their diet consisted of fish and shellfish as they made their way farther and farther south. As the ice receded and the land opened up, these early people began to spread out across the continent. Early prehistoric people used stone tools and made spear and arrow points that are quite identifiable. One such group is called the Clovis People.

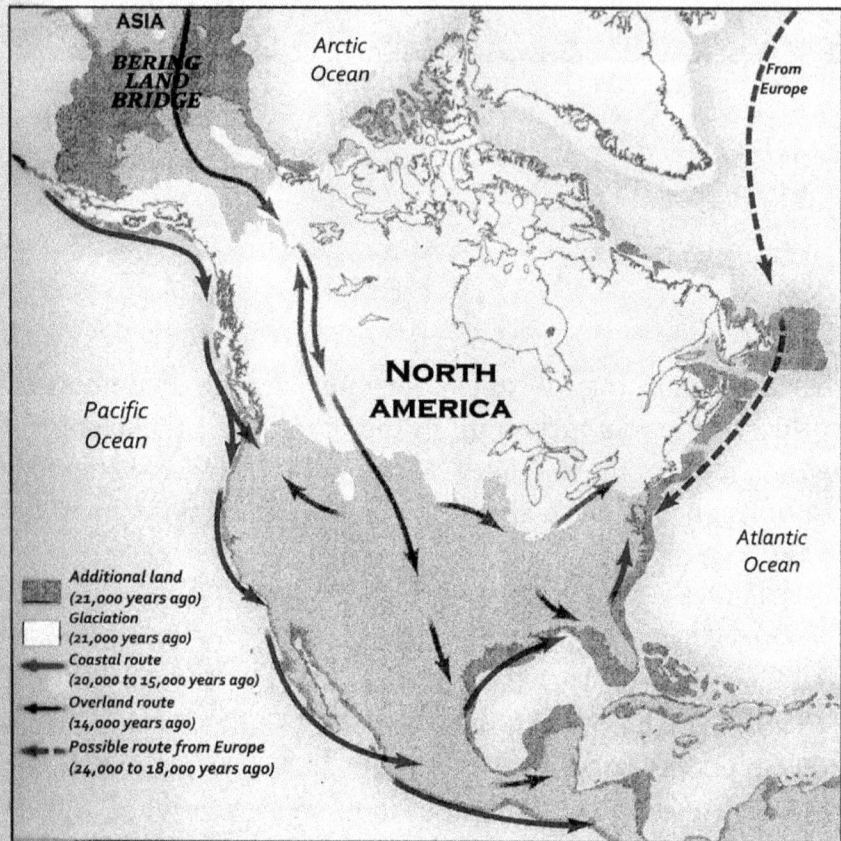

ASIA

BERING
LAND
BRIDGE

Arctic
Ocean

From
Europe

Pacific
Ocean

NORTH
AMERICA

Atlantic
Ocean

Additional land
(21,000 years ago)
Glaciation
(21,000 years ago)
Coastal route
(20,000 to 15,000 years ago)
Overland route
(14,000 years ago)
Possible route from Europe
(24,000 to 18,000 years ago)

Migration Routes

This map shows the Bering Land Bridge that connected Asia to North America during the most recent Ice Age when sea levels were low. The earliest people to populate the American Continents may have walked across the land bridge and then southward in search of food and new habitat. Some may have arrived by boat following routes along the extended coastlines. Migration then spread to the continent interior.

A dig site in the small town of Clovis, New Mexico during the 1920s revealed a treasure trove of artifacts. The Clovis point was a distinctly shaped spear and arrow point that was flaked along their length on both sides. Similar points and tools were found in northeastern Asia which led scientists to believe that these were the people who crossed the land bridge over the Bering Straight and settled across the North and South American continents. The theory was called the *Clovis First*, meaning that these Clovis people were the first to settle in the Americas. But a chance discovery in Chile near the tip of South America changed all of that. Radiocarbon dating of the site at Monte Verde showed it to be around 14,600 years old. This places people in that site over a thousand years before the Clovis people.

About the same time the Chile dig was taking place, scientists were digging in caves in Pennsylvania called the *Meadowcroft Rockshelter*; radiocarbon dating of the tools discovered there showed they were at least 16,000 years old— much older than Clovis

Additional dig sites at South Carolina, Texas and Brazil led scientists to believe that the Clovis First theory was in error. Recently, scientists have found evidence in the *Paisley Caves* of Oregon that has led them to conclude that humans were present in North America at least a thousand years before the Clovis people arrived. These earlier people had no technological or genetic similarity to the Clovis people. So, there were people here longer than thought, but the new question is where did they come from and how did they reach America?

Did they cross the Bering Land Bridge or did they arrive in boats? Did they cross the Atlantic or Pacific oceans? So far those questions have not been answered.

Archeologists have much to learn. Suffice it to say there are many sites across the continent where pre-historic settlements have been found. This means that the people who traveled here spread out across the entire country and some of them settled in the region that is now Wisconsin. These early people were primarily mobile hunters and gatherers. They hunted large game such as mammoth and mastodon. Later they hunted bison, elk, and deer. Fish and shellfish were also in their diet.

It's hard to imagine a mastodon lumbering along in the Wisconsin terrain, but they surely were here and evidence of their presence has been found. In July of 1897, the Dosch brothers—Harry, Chris, Verne and Clyde—were checking for flood damage along Mill Creek near the village of Boaz, Wisconsin after a big rainstorm that had flooded the small stream. Boaz is about ten miles from the Wisconsin River along the upper part of Mill Creek. The boys found some unusual bones sticking out of the creek bank where it had been partially washed away by the high water. Being typical boys, they dug the bones out of the mud and put them on display by a hitching post at the road that ran past their farm. Mailmen quickly spread the news of the find across the area. Local newspapers ran stories of the unusual artifacts, and it didn't take long for a lawyer who was a member of the state legislature to negotiate a sale of the bones to the State of Wisconsin for fifty dollars. From the 2/3 complete skeleton reconstructed in 1915 and housed in the Geology Museum at the University of Wisconsin, it is estimated that the mastodon was a bit over 9 feet tall and 18 feet long and weighed between six and eight tons.

Boaz mastodon skeleton
(Photo by Ron Nagel)

When the bones were found, the boys also found a spear point in the area of the rib bones. This point did not accompany the bones when they were shipped to Madison, but in the 1940s the University received an envelope containing a quartzite spear point. The envelope was from D. Dosch who lived in Missouri. Two of the surviving Dosch brothers identified the spear point as being the one they'd found over 60 years earlier. A note with the spear point simply said, *"Allegedly found with the U.W. elephant."*

While it is commonly thought that the mastodon became extinct at the end of the ice age 11,000 years ago, many think they were still alive much later, as recent as 8,000 or 10,000 years ago. One possibility of mastodons living in the Wisconsin area much later than they did in other areas is that this part of the world was never glaciated. During the time that the rest of the northern hemisphere was covered in a mile of ice, the Wisconsin River valley and the rest of the Driftless Area were much as they are today. It was most likely much cooler and the summers were very short, but life was possible here while it was impossible in many other places. This makes the idea of a mastodon living here much later than they did in other places more plausible. It also stands to reason that many ancient people lived in the area during the Ice Ages. The Driftless Area was like an ark in the middle of a vast sea of ice; life for people and animals could have been sustained here, unlike any other place in the northern part of the world.

Archeologists have discovered solid evidence of people living in the Wisconsin River area for ten thousand years or more. They classify them by the times they lived, lifestyles, the tools they used, and their methods of burying their dead.

The earliest people to occupy the region were *Paleo-Indians*. They were largely hunter/gatherers who migrated to the area in small bands or groups with organized leadership that assigned jobs to the members most suited for certain tasks. These people used projectiles such as Clovis points for hunting game.

The period of around six thousand years ago is designated as the *Early Archaic* stage. Occupants of this era were probably related to the people who first came to the vicinity but had evolved their technology to a much higher degree, determined by the type of projectile points and other developments in tools and hunting tactics. Fishing gear was being utilized; copper tools were being manufactured; milling stones were used to process food. The first appearance of domestic dogs shows up during this time, and there is evidence of long distance trade networks being developed.

About 500BC the practice of mound building developed. This stage is called the *Woodland Tradition*. These people were very widespread across the area near the Wisconsin River. They left behind hundreds of mounds that are very important in the story of Paul Seifert and his days living in the area. Other advancements associated with this culture include the use of sand or grit in the making of ceramic pottery, and the development of horticulture.

The Mound Builders were much more advanced than the later people who would settle the area. The creations they left behind are typically called Indian Mounds, but actually, they were built by a race of people that was here even before our Indians. The mounds are repositories for pottery, tools, arrowheads, spearheads, scrapers, and stone axes. Some contained beads, and often were the final resting place for the dead. They were built in many shapes and sizes from small conical mounds ten to fifteen feet across, to huge replicas of animals up to three hundred feet long. Some of them were shaped like beaver, bison, or birds, while others were shaped like snakes and turtles.

One curious thing about the mounds is that they were not built with the soil from the immediate surrounding area. In most cases they are built on a smooth level area, but the dirt used in their construction was brought in from someplace else, probably carried in with baskets.

Many of the mounds have been eroded away and are no longer visible. If they happened to be in a farm field, they were plowed over time and time again until they blended in with the rest of the field and were lost. The majority of the mounds were built near waterways, many along the Wisconsin River, but most are camouflaged by trees and brush growing over them making them difficult to detect. However, there are numerous surviving mounds still clearly visible; one such example is that of *Effigy Mound*, a bird shaped mound easily viewed from Hwy 60 about one mile west of its intersection with Hwy 80 in Richland County. *Effigy Mound* is one of a large group consisting of about 75 mounds that lie along the Wisconsin River known as the *Ghost Eagle Site*. Approximately 20 of these mounds are bird or eagle shapes, quite visible in years past, but unfortunately, they were in the middle of large farm fields; over many seasons of plowing, most have been obliterated and are no longer visible. Fortunately, they were mapped in the late 1800s; these old maps show a great diversity of shapes and sizes.

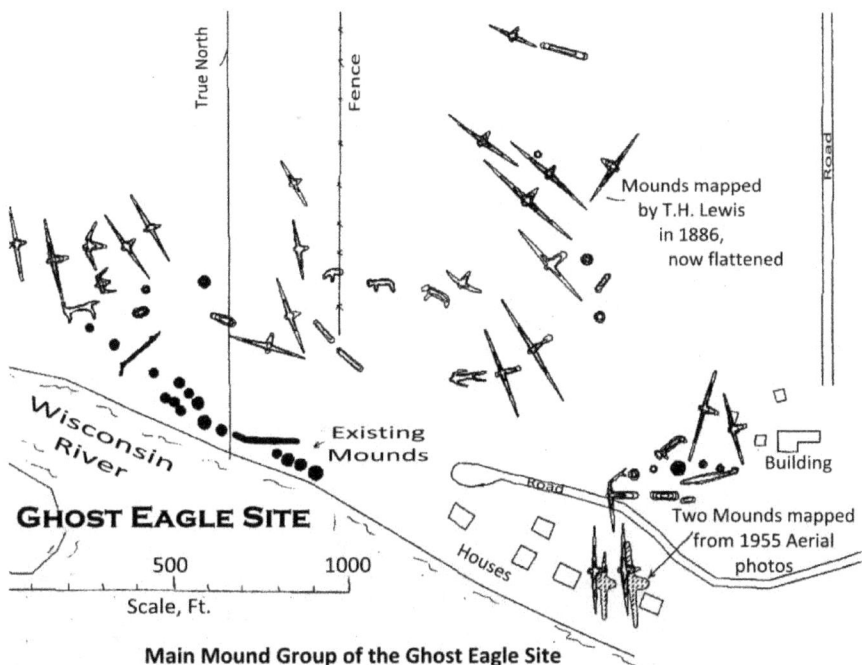

Main Mound Group of the Ghost Eagle Site

There are two more spectacular mound groups near the *Ghost Eagle Site* known as *Hill East* and *Hill West*. And here is where the story gets really interesting. The mounds on *Hill East*, (also known as Frank's Hill, in honor the late Frank Shadewald who was caretaker of them for many years) are intact and well preserved. At the crest of the hill on the east end is the first mound in the shape of a snake. The next mound is a beaver or lodge mound. Then there is a bird shaped mound, a bison mound and a coyote mound. Frank has burned the brush and mowed the area so the mounds are incredibly visible and well preserved.

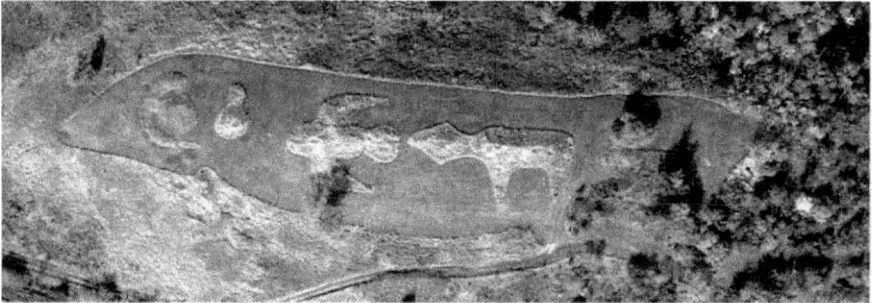

Aerial photo view of Hill East

Aerial photo view of Hill West

Across the valley at the top of *Hill West* is a string of 12 round mounds that stretch from north to south; at first glance they mean nothing. But in fact, they are markers for the seasons and times to plant crops, laid out by ancient people, as interpreted in 2009 by Ralph Redfox, a Cheyenne elder. His visit to the site answered many questions of the site's mystery.

If you stand on the highest point of *Hill East*, on the tail of the bird mound, you have before you a functional solar calendar as the setting sun aligns with each mound on *Hill West*.

This calendar would function from the end of April to the summer solstice, and then until mid-August, the time from planting to harvest.

Redfox observed and recognized a fire pit, which consists of 14 stones. It represents the places of the spirits and the Creator. On the right side, the stones of the four keepers and three caretakers. The four keepers are the directions, north, south, east and west. The three caretakers are deep earth, earth's surface and the atmosphere.

The left side represents what is here on earth: plant life, aquatic life, animals with feathers, animals with two legs, animals with four legs, animals underground, and medicinal plants.

Mr. Redfox identified the snake mound as the feathered serpent, *Quetzal Coltal*, a Mayan god. He also identified the bird mound as not a bird, but as *The Corn Lady*. The Corn Lady legend was passed down to Mr. Redfox by his grandparents. They learned the stories from the ancient storytellers:

Many winters ago after the ice melted and the animals had left the area, the people lived in marshes. They survived eating fish and birds. One day in the camp there was a game of hoop being played. As one of the young men approached the group he noticed a man on the other side of the game dressed the same as himself. He approached the other man and the stranger said that his outfit came from the cave under the spring. They challenged each other and went to the spring followed by a crowd.

Now they went into the cave and there sat an old lady. She was cooking corn in one pot and bison in another. She called out, "Come my grandson and eat." They ate until they were full but the food did not run out. The old lady said, "This is my gift for you. Take it back to camp."

The two young men took the corn and bison back to camp and everyone ate but the food did not run out. They were given instructions on how and when to plant the corn, and how to use the bison. This would be their food thereafter. From then on they grew corn, and one day woke to witness the bison coming, filling the whole valley.

In the spring, the time of planting was given to them by standing on the highest point—the tail of the bird, or the womb of the corn lady—and when the sun set on the first mound across the valley, it told them that it was time to plant the corn. The setting sun also lines up precisely with other Ghost Eagle mounds, indicating the summer and winter solstice.

Did these mound builders have contact with the Mayans? Were there Mayans in the Wisconsin River valley? Was the use of the feathered serpent mound a coincidence? These are interesting and unanswered questions.

The practice of erecting monuments to the dead wasn't uncommon. The same rituals were practiced at the same time in Egypt resulting in the pyramids. The Aztecs, Mayans, and Incas built huge monuments similar to the pyramids in Central America. In other cultures all over the world there are mounds, some of them of colossal size, erected by similar peoples.

Mounds at crest of Hill East are clearly visible from Hwy 193. (Photo by Dan Bomkamp)

Paul Seifert mapped the mounds in a two square mile area in another mound-abundant site at the confluence of the Pine and Wisconsin Rivers, about three miles east of Bogus Bluff. There can be no doubt that the Mound Builders were present at the mouth of the Pine River for thousands of years. Seifert identified and mapped over seventy-five mounds in that area alone. Thousands of other artifacts have been discovered there that indicate that this was a very advanced society. For example, sites have been found where they worked at making spear and arrow points. In these workshops there are two separate areas: one containing large chips that were first taken off the stone, and one containing fine chips. The piles of large chips show that some were not skilled enough to make perfect points, so their job was to prepare the piece for the more skilled workers. At the second pile, much smaller chips show that this was where the skilled artisans of the tribe refined the

points to a perfect projectile ready to use. This indicates that these people had divided into different classes, based on varying levels of skill.

The Mound Builders existed in large numbers; they were extremely intelligent and advanced in their culture. But then, for some unknown reason they disappeared, leaving no trace of their coming or going. They died out rapidly, and because they had no written language, they left no names, no traditions, and almost nothing of their existence except the mounds. The same fate came to the Mayans. Is there a connection?

When the mound builders were gone the early Indians—our Native Americans—eventually took their place. They were not as advanced as the mound builders, but they inhabited the same places, near rivers and streams, where their predecessors had lived.

Regardless of which archeological stage or name given to it by scientists, the fact is that there may have been people living in the Bogus Bluff area for ten thousand years or more, considering the possibility of the Clovis people migrating this far east. A 1998 archeological survey at the site of a new bridge construction on State Highway 60 over the Pine River at Gotham, Wisconsin uncovered nearly 80,000 artifacts from eleven holes equaling 126 square meters. Artifacts from several levels were cataloged, consisting of pottery shards, projectile points, tools, and beads. This dig was nearly a mile from where many mounds were built nearer the Wisconsin River. It was concluded that the Pine River site, where the Pine flows into the Wisconsin, was a continual human habitat for over 6,000 years. That means there were people living there in 4,000 BC. When considering that the pyramids were built about 2,500 BC, it illustrates just how long people have inhabited this river valley.

Just a stone's throw away across the river from this site is the *Gottschall Rock Shelter* site in Iowa County, on the south side of the river. The site was excavated and studied for nearly 20 years by Doctor Robert Salzer and Grace Rajnovich from Beloit College. The site is not a cave, but a rock overhang that was used from about 300 AD to the early Nineteenth Century. In an interview by this author, Dr. Salzer stated that the site was like a "wayside" for ancient peoples. Travelers from near and far knew of it and took advantage of its sheltering characteristics when traveling through this area during hunting or trading expeditions. Rock art images have found there telling a legend of the *Ioway* and *Ho-Chunk* people. These Siouan-speaking tribes originated along the East Coast of the North American Continent, but by the time of European explorers' first contact, the *Ho-Chunk* had migrated to the Great Lakes region, and the *Ioway* to what is now the state of Iowa. Also at this site, a sculpted and painted stone head was found with ties to the *Mississippian Culture*, a mound building society that transitioned from the *Late Woodlands*, and Southern cult motifs from all over North America.

While digging down through the layers at the *Gottschall* site, archeologists have found bones of ancient animals, as well as those of ancient humans. One very common find is small pieces of skulls about the size of a quarter. Dozens of these skull fragments have been found at the site, but never a complete skull. The skull pieces had distinct amounts of the element Strontium, an alkaline earth element, in their makeup. Measurements of Strontium in the soil are very specific for an area. By analyzing the skull fragments, Dr. Salzer and his team found that the bones were a match to the site near Lake Mills, Wisconsin called *Aztalan*. The *Aztalan* site is that of the *Mississipian Culture*, occupied during the Tenth to Thirteenth Centuries. The people of this culture constructed huge mounds used for religious and political purposes and are known for their widespread trading routes.

How did the skull fragments of people living at *Aztalan* get to the *Gottchall* Site? We will probably never know; it's just one more of the many mysteries of the Lower Wisconsin River.

Something that all of the sites of long habitation have in common is that they are near smaller tributaries of the Wisconsin River. In addition to the Pine River site, there are sites at Mill Creek, Willow Creek, and Knapps Creek. So, when one asks how could so many artifacts and so many skeletons actually exist in the Burial Chamber at Bogus Bluff, the answer is clear. There were people living nearby for 6,000 years. If the cave is really there, it most likely had an opening near the bottom of the hill that offered easy entrance to the chamber. No doubt, that entrance has collapsed and was somehow lost, sealing the skeletons and artifacts inside until Seifert *may* have found another entrance higher up. There were certainly enough people living in and traveling through the area to fill the place with bodies and treasure.

"Friends, I cannot describe the horror I felt. The bottom of the cave is covered with skeletons of a vanished race. Skulls are everywhere. Here perished a tribe, very near I should say, a nation."

This is an excerpt from the Von Wolfgang *Rose Colored Spear* letter published after his visit to Paul Seifert at Richland City. While the letter doesn't give us an actual number, it seems that there were hundreds, if not thousands, of skulls and bones in the Indian Burial Cave. Who were these people? When did they live here? How did their bones get into this deep dark cave? Those are some of the questions that make Paul Seifert's discovery such a mystery. His story is very similar to that of Eagle Cave. It also tells of a huge cavern filled with the bones of hundreds, or maybe thousands of people. So the story of Paul Seifert's discovery is *possible*. But is it real... or just the same story re-told?

Caves...
Archeological Storehouses

As long as there have been humans on earth, they have used caves as shelters, places of worship and places to bury their dead. They have recorded their way of life in pictographs on cave walls, the animals they hunted and the gods they worshipped. There are thousands of caves around the world. One in South Africa holds evidence of human habitation 60,000 years ago.

The longest cave found to date is *Mammoth Cave* in Kentucky. It is 390 miles in length. The deepest cave is in the former Soviet State of Georgia; *Voronya Cave* is 7,188 feet deep, measured from its entrance to the deepest point. A cave in Malaysia has the largest room called the *Sarawak Chamber*. It measures approximately 23,000 feet by 1,300 feet with a ceiling height of 260 feet.

Caves are found in all parts of the world and have been formed in several ways. The formation and development of caves is a process called *speleogenesis*, and a person who explores caves for scientific purposes or recreation is called a spelunker. There are several processes that form caves. These processes result in Solutional Caves, Primary Caves, Sea Caves,

Corrasional Caves, Glacier Caves, and Anchialine Caves.

Caves in Wisconsin for the most part are Solutional Caves. This means they are caves that are formed in rock that is soluble. In areas where the rock is marble, or granite, caves will not form because of the hardness of the rock. But in areas where the rock is limestone, chalk, dolomite or gypsum, the rock is dissolved over the centuries by rainwater and natural acid in groundwater that seeps through the faults and joints. Little by little, tiny openings form in the rock as water seeps through these tiny cracks every time it rains. These cracks eventually widen and after many centuries, the soft limestone and other soft stone is dissolved leaving the harder rock that forms the walls of the cave.

A similar process is common in many places resulting in sinkholes. Florida is known for these sinkholes that sometimes swallow up homes, parking lots and highways. They are the result of veins of limestone in the bedrock that dissolve over the centuries due to the high water table; suddenly the topsoil gives away and falls into the abyss below it.

The largest and most often discovered Solutional Caves are found in areas rich in limestone. Rainwater and groundwater charged with carbonic acid dissolves the limestone over the centuries. Carbonic acid is a weak acid created by the addition of carbon dioxide to water. It is the same acid that is in carbonated water used in soda to create the fizz. Though carbonic acid is weak, it does its work hour after hour, day after day for thousands of years and the result is a cave that may be anything from a small crack to a huge twisting trail through the earth.

Many caves have primitive drawings made by ancient man depicting life in long gone ages. Others hold treasures left behind by people who lived there centuries ago. While not valuable like gold or silver, spearheads or pottery shards are simple things that tell us the story of life thousands of years in the past. Often, the most interesting part of a cave is its garbage dump; pieces of broken pottery, broken arrow points, bones of animals, and other "garbage" of the ancient people reveals the lifestyles of past centuries. Scientists often find fossilized seeds that tell us of the plants that grew in ancient times. A tiny scrap of what was garbage to the ancient people is a valuable element in determining how ancient man lived.

Cave opening at Bogus Bluff (Photos by Jolene Newkirk)

Bogus Bluff

Two things that naturally go together are caves and treasure. Folklore connected with nearly every cave that man has crawled into involves treasure, lost artifacts, skeletons, mystery. Bogus Bluff is a place with not just one treasure story—it has many.

About three miles west of Gotham, Wisconsin along the Wisconsin River and Hwy 60 is located a lofty bluff with rock outcroppings where an ancient cave, not visible from the roadway, has mystified explorers and scientists for decades. Its legacy includes the many tales from as far back as the 1700s when the cliffs were frequented by Indians, fur traders, outlaws, and farmers using the Wisconsin River as the easiest access to this land. The bluff-top was an excellent place to watch travelers on the River; outlaws considered Bogus Bluff an excellent hiding place.

Above Hwy 60 is a steep, south facing slope, heavily forested with oak, aspen, red maple, hickory, white pine, and white birch. It is habitat for abundant wildlife such as whip-poor-will, great horned owls, white-tailed deer, rattlesnakes, sand hill cranes, bats, and many more species of animals. Near the top is the rock cliff and cave openings, some 250 feet above the river surface.

How did Bogus Bluff get its unusual name?

There are two stories about that. The first is that early settlers to the area noticed the yellow rock face of the bluff while traveling on the Wisconsin River, and were attracted to it because it looked like gold. They climbed the bluff and dug for many weeks finding nothing but rock, finally declaring *"That it was a Bogus Bluff with no gold in it."*

Others claim that the name Bogus Bluff originated with counterfeiters who used the caves as their hideout just after the Civil War. They supposedly produced counterfeit (bogus) $20 bills in a part of the cave that they enlarged into a room where they worked and lived. Part of this story implies that Federal agents got wind of the counterfeiting ring and raided the Bogus Bluff hideout, but the counterfeiters managed to escape through a hidden entrance, and then led the agents down the river in a boat chase. The Feds finally captured the bad guys, but they had tossed their printing plates into the river. They were taken to Boscobel, put on trial, convicted, and sent to prison. Because of the counterfeiting practice carried out on that hill, the place was named Bogus Bluff after the fake or bogus bills made there.

There is indeed a room in the hillside that is most likely where this legend was born. When one enters the opening in the front of the bluff, he finds a passage that leads deep into the hill. This passage branches off to a short cave that emerges on the side of the hill, and a much longer passage that continues for about 450 feet, emerging on the west part of the hill near the top. When an explorer comes out of that long, narrow tunnel into the bright sunlight, it's a wonderful feeling. Once eyes are adjusted to the light, the panoramic view of the river valley is utterly breathtaking.

Between these passages is that short cave that ends in the room carved out of the rock. The ceiling is blackened, probably with the smoke and soot from candles or lanterns for lighting, suggesting that it may have been a workshop and sleeping quarters.

Author's note: Many years ago I crawled into this room and tried to imagine working and sleeping in such a place. The walls have been chipped away to make the room larger, and the ceiling is indeed blackened. It seems that there is fresh air in the chamber, so there must be cracks leading to the outside, making it possible for someone to work or live in it. After spending only a few minutes there, I decided it would be the last place I'd want to live. But for a counterfeiter, it certainly made an excellent hideout. D.B.

Counterfeiters contributed a significant mark in Midwestern history in the later years of the Nineteenth Century. The Wisconsin cities of Boscobel and Monroe were the centers of the counterfeiting industry in the Midwest. The kingpin was Napoleon Bonaparte Latta leading a ring of counterfeiters who made fake money that only experts could distinguish from the real thing. It was believed that Latta had stolen the printing plates from the U.S. Treasury, and his fake bills were as perfect as any ever made.

Federal authorities arrested Latta at his Monroe, Wisconsin home in 1871. Counterfeit money was found buried in his yard at the time of his arrest; however, the printing plates had disappeared. Two of Latta's counterfeiting cohorts were also caught, but his right-hand man, Charles "Pent" Ellis managed to escape arrest.

Ellis had been the distributor for the fake money. He would contact dishonest people willing to buy the fake bills with real money. They received several dollars of fake bills in return for every dollar of real money.

About the same time Latta was captured, the Miner and Cole counterfeiting gang of New York was broken up. Three members of that gang—brothers, Tom, Bob, and George Ballard—escaped arrest and fled to Iowa. They soon met Ellis and his "Green-backers" gang and entered into business.

In the fall of 1878, local people of the Bogus Bluff vicinity became aware that the Alfred Beckwith family had four strangers visiting them. Beckwith told his neighbors that they were wealthy men who were there hunting and fishing, and that they were his wife's relatives.

Beckwith's home was near the road in the shadow of Bogus Bluff. A long, narrow ravine separated Beckwith's house from the next bluff to the east, and nearby was the home of Paul Seifert.

According to legend, Seifert observed the four strangers hike up the hill past his house on numerous occasions. They never seemed to be hunting, nor did they really appear to be doing anything of note; they just seemed to like roaming over the bluffs. Sometimes they'd disappear and he'd not see them for many days.

Then one day he saw them carrying a large, wooden chest up the hill that appeared to be quite heavy. About this same time, strange lights were observed at the top of Bogus Bluff. Similar lights burned on other high points up and down the river; the lights seemed to be signals sent by whoever was responsible for this strange activity. Answering flashes of light came from Bald Point in Iowa County across the river, sometimes from Point Jude near Lone Rock, and on clear nights there were lights on Point Judas, which overlooked the shot tower at Helena, and from Blue Mounds.

As the men came and went, local residents learned their names to be Tom, Bob, and George Ballard, and Charles "Pent" Ellis, but these names meant nothing to them.

Paul was known as a generous man who often took in wayfarers, sheltered and fed them. One evening Paul was walking home from Richland City when he saw a very old man sitting on a stone next to the river. Paul asked him why he was there. The man replied that he had no home, so Paul took the old man with him to his house. When asked, the man told Paul that he had no friends, nor did he have any money. He said he was heading west where he owned some land.

The man stayed for a week and almost never went outdoors. He seemed interested in all things but wasn't very talkative. Then one evening, Beckwith told Paul that one of the Ballard brothers wanted to talk to him. During the resulting conversation, Ballard asked a lot of questions about the old man, but Paul knew little about him. The next morning the old man left.

About a week later, a vicious gun battle broke out near Bogus Bluff. There had been some Indians camping nearby, so Paul thought it might be them fighting with some local men who were not fond of Indians.

When the smoke cleared, Paul learned that five U.S. Marshals on the trail of Pent Ellis and his gang had arrived at Lone Rock via the train from Madison. They had attacked the gang at Bogus Bluff.

Sometime later, Paul was walking down the road when a young man in a buggy offered him a ride. Paul declined since he liked walking, but the man insisted. He had information that Paul would find interesting.

Paul was surprised to learn that he had been the *old man* who Paul had taken into his home. He had been looking for counterfeiters, and because Paul had bought a quantity of green paint, he felt obligated to investigate. When the man saw Paul's paintings in his home, he knew Paul wasn't the counterfeiter, but when he learned of the four strangers climbing the hill nearly every day, and their names, he put the scheme together; he was sure he had solved the case. Unfortunately, instead of capturing the gang, the raid only resulted in scaring off the counterfeiters.

Another version of this episode is told by S.W. Fogo, editor of the *Republican Observer* at Richland Center in the early 1900s, who knew most of the old men living in the area at the time of the Bogus Bluff counterfeiting days. According to Mr. Fogo, the band of counterfeiters escaped capture during the Bogus Bluff raid through a secret passageway, and none of the bogus money was found; it was believed that the outlaws buried it there. However, three of the most notorious fake money makers were captured a few miles downriver at Boscobel in 1878. Whether they had any connection with the men on Bogus Bluff was not known.

A Treasure in Gold

There are several tales of secreted treasures in the passages of Bogus Bluff. One tells of a wealth in gold coins hidden somewhere in the caves early in the Nineteenth Century. John Jacob Astor, a German immigrant who came to America after the Revolutionary War became involved with the fur trading business, quickly recognizing a way to make huge profits shipping beaver, otter and mink pelts to Europe. Once treaties were made with Canada, he became a leading fur trader there, and later when the Great Lakes region opened for fur trading, he was the first to set up trading posts, making a fortune by trading with the Indians and local trappers.

As was the case in all places in the wilderness at that time, rivers were the main highways used for travel and trade. Astor was active in the Great Lakes area and sent traders up the Fox River to where the Fox and Wisconsin Rivers are only two miles apart. There they portaged to the Wisconsin and found their way to the Mississippi, establishing a trading post at Prairie du Chien in what would someday be Wisconsin.

Each spring Astor would send his men with canoes up the Fox, cross to the Wisconsin, and there they built a large raft to transport a large sum in gold coins to the trading post at Prairie du Chien. This would be the money used to buy furs for a year. At the end of each season the furs were hauled back up the river, and new money was sent back for the next year's business.

There was very little domestic money in those times, so coins from other countries were used for trading in America. A popular coin of the times was the 20 Franc Bonaparte, a French coin that was about 1/5 ounce of gold. Gold was worth $19 per ounce at that time; a Bonaparte was worth about four dollars. Today they are worth nearly $400 each. There seems to be no record of how many gold coins were in the shipment, but if there was enough money for a year of trading, it must have been a large amount. At today's gold prices it would amount to, perhaps, millions of dollars.

As the story has been passed on, Astor's men were traveling down the river when they reached a spot they knew to be *"About four days paddle from Prairie du Chien."* There a band of Indians attacked the raft. Astor's men battled bravely but were defeated. Most were killed; one survivor, however, managed to hide in tall grass and watched as the Indians maneuvered the raft to shore, removed the gold, and set the raft afire, allowing it to drift downriver on the current until it burned and sank. Then the man observed the Indians "carrying the gold up a tremendously high bluff and disappearing into a cave." When it appeared that the Indians had left, he came out of hiding and made his way to Prairie du Chien and safety.

Bogus Bluff is just four days paddle from Prairie du Chien, and is the only bluff with a high, visible cave entrance.

There is another similar legend involving the Spanish military.

Spain had a major presence in America in early times with garrisons in the Great Lakes region and all the way down the Mississippi River to New Orleans. This story involves yet another shipment of gold coins, this time being shipped to the New Orleans garrison to pay the soldiers. Again, the troops carrying the gold paddled up the Fox River, portaged to the Wisconsin River, and then began their journey to the Mississippi River that would eventually land them at New Orleans.

The Spanish soldiers experienced a similar attack and met the same fate as the fur traders' expedition. Once again, the Indians overpowered the soldiers and took the gold, depositing the large quantity of Spanish Doubloons into a cave. A Doubloon was about the same worth as the French coins—about four dollars each.

A third story is that of river pirates that terrorized travelers on the Wisconsin for many years. In those days any navigable waterway was subject to the plight of pirates. Since rivers were the main mode of travel, pirates took advantage of the fact and preyed on those journeying up or down the rivers. This time the army was transporting "good American Dollars" from Green Bay to the garrison at Fort Crawford near Prairie du Chien. Pirates attacked the rafts and overwhelmed the couriers, climbed up the tall bluff and disappeared into a cave with their loot.

So we have three very similar stories that could be true, or maybe they're just stories. Because they are so similar could mean that one of them may be true and the others have been derived from the original. Over the years many people have searched and dug for the gold and found nothing. There have been psychics who thought they could find the gold, Cornish miners from Mineral Point who dug side tunnels looking for a hidden passage, and there was even a group with ground penetrating radar who thought they could find the gold by imaging it with the machine.

The steep climb up to the cave is very difficult and dangerous, and there is always a good chance of encountering a rattlesnake on the way.   Hundreds of people have crawled through the tunnels over the years and it's a great experience. One of the tunnels has been mapped by a group of spelunkers and found to be nearly 450 feet long. It's not a place for someone who is claustrophobic.

The cave is on private land and has been owned by the same family since 1947. Because of damaging abuse to the property, the family does not allow anyone to explore the cave without permission. They are simply trying to protect and preserve the site.

Bogus Bluff has many stories to choose from for the origin of its name, and legends are plentiful about gold treasures and a Burial Cave. Are any of the tales true? It's hard to say for sure. But one fact is for certain: Bogus Bluff is a place wrapped in mystery.

The Pine River Delta

The Pine River today is a stream that varies from 15 to 20 feet wide with a depth of 2 to 7 feet. It wouldn't seem possible that this little trout stream could have formed the delta at its mouth where it meets the Wisconsin River, but it did. Thousands of tons of sand, clay and mud were washed down the Pine River valley that formed the delta, but it happened gradually over thousands of years.

Richland County is blessed with miles and miles of small streams. Many of them are fine trout streams that drain the county to the Wisconsin River. Many of these streams are in the mid to eastern part of the county and they all feed into the Pine River. The Pine starts in Vernon County and flows south into the northern part of Richland County where it meets the West Branch of the Pine. From there on, small feeder streams flow into it and it grows. Ash Creek, Brush Creek, Horse Creek, Fancy Creek, Little Willow, Willow, and others all become one stream—the Pine.

Today most of these feeders are nothing but tiny trickles of water that can be jumped over most of the year. How could these few small streams create a mile square delta? The answer lies in the ancient history, at the time of glacial melting and the catastrophic failure of the dam containing Glacial Lake Wisconsin. All that water flowed across Southern Wisconsin— a large portion down the Pine and its tributaries—into the Wisconsin River valley.

Rock formations at Rockbridge show clearly the evidence of water erosion that occurred thousands of years ago. (Photos by Dan Bomkamp)

A drive through Richland County on State Highway 80 or 58 reveals many examples of hillsides that have been scoured away by water, leaving striations in the rocks and amazing features like Elephant Trunk Rock, (Above photos, lower right) and Rockbridge Natural Bridge (Upper left). This is clear evidence that an enormous amount of water flowed through this area; the little streams that meandered through the valleys turned into raging rivers, pushing tons of silt and mud and sand into the Pine, and eventually all that material settled out when it reached the broad Wisconsin River valley forming the large delta at the mouth of the Pine. This happened over a period of many years, and as the water was eventually drained from the north, these streams settled back into their banks and the Pine became a stream again.

The enormous quantity of sand, clay and dirt deposited at the mouth of the Pine developed into a flat fertile plain, an inviting place where the people who settled there could grow crops, fish, hunt and build their villages. Various cultures including the Mound Builders occupied the area for thousands of years and left behind mounds, burial sites and countless spear points, axe heads, and other fragments of their cultures. The land was elevated to provide safety from flooding, and adequately fertile to make it a wonderful place to live. Centuries later, men looking for a place to start a settlement looked at this flat, fertile land and decided it was where they would build their town, Richland City.

1895
PLAT OF
BUENA VISTA
Townships 8 & 9 North. Ranges 1 & 2 East.
of the 4th Principal Meridian
RICHLAND COUNTY, WIS

Richland City

The first pioneer took up residence in what is now known as Richland County in 1840. His name was John Coumbe, a bachelor Englishman who built a log cabin near present day Port Andrew. Later that year another family settled in what is now called Eagle Corners. That fall three more pioneers, W.H. Waters, his brother Samuel and William Smiley lived with Coumbe until the following spring, when they forged their way up Byrd's Creek and established claims there. Several years later, 1848, they desired to expand their game hunting territory; the Waters brothers and two others canoed up the Wisconsin River from Port Andrews to the mouth of the Pine River, and then paddled up the Pine to Ash Creek where they established hunting and trapping camps.

The McCloud brothers were early settlers in what is now the Town of Buena Vista. They established claims near Bear Creek. One of the enduring legends of the Bogus Bluff area is that of Judith McCloud, a sister. It seems that Judith was out roaming the bluffs, picking berries or looking for some other bounty when she encountered some local Indians. Rather than be captured and taken hostage by the Indians, Judith ran to the end of the bluff and hurled herself off the cliff and was killed. To this day, the spot is known as Judith's Point.

It is fact that there were two McCloud brothers who hated Indians and supposedly killed many of them over the years. Some say it was in retaliation for the death of their sister, Judith, and others say no. More recent relatives of the McCloud family claim there never was a Judith McCloud. Whichever is true, the account of Judith's Point is one of the long-lasting legends of the Bogus Bluff area.

Travel in that time was over footpaths made by the Indians or along game trails, or the most common way of travel, by water. Two enterprising pioneers, John Smith and Thomas Mathews established a ferry between Muscoda and the north side of the Wisconsin River in a place they called Richmond, which later became Orion. It was the first town platted in Richland County.

Samuel Swinehart crossed the river at Muscoda in 1843 and made his way up the Pine River to establish a camp on its east bank. The local Indians claimed the land as their territory, so Swinehart was soon compelled to move farther up the Pine, exploring the valley where the west branch flowed through a high sandstone ridge; there he found the famous natural bridge at what is now Rockbridge, eight miles north of Richland Center.

Swinehart spent many days in the area examining and assessing the abundant pine forest (for which the Pine River was named); he could foresee his own wealth if he were to cut the timber and deliver it to a lumber mill. He made a careful study and determined that the stream was suitable for moving the logs. Swinehart made his first claim and built a cabin. The following year, 1844, he built a sawmill, and cleared the Pine River of downed trees and other obstructions, making it possible to raft the pine lumber to the Wisconsin River.

To further enrich his enterprise, Swinehart built a lumberyard the next year on the south side of the Wisconsin where present day Avoca Lake runs into the river, a place now called Blue Lake. The ferry at Laws Landing, which was just downriver a short distance, connected his lumberyard with the north side of the river. For the next few years, structures in the towns of Highland, Mineral Point and Dodgeville were built with lumber that came from Swinehart's lumberyard, originating at the Rockbridge mill.

But Swinehart soon sold the lumber yard to a man from Galena, with intentions of enlarging his Rockbridge sawmill and expanding lumber production. He hired a crew, bought supplies, and after a difficult, week-long journey, they arrived at Rockbridge. With the onset of winter and deep snow, they had been forced to leave the oxen teams and wagons at Orion, and had continued the voyage with sleds via the frozen Indian Creek. (Indian Creek today is but a trickle of water that can be stepped across at almost any point along it course.) Timber cutting continued at the Rockbridge pine forest, and with the mill expansion complete, it did a thriving business in the following years.

The spring of 1848 found Isaac Wallace and his partner, Garwood Green, at the confluence of the Pine and Wisconsin Rivers in search of a location for a proposed town. With its high, flat, fertile ground, well above the flood plain, and at the juncture of two water routes, it seemed the perfect location for a commercial port. Wallace and Green staked their claim on this site that would be called Richland City. They bought the land the following spring, and that summer it was surveyed and platted in 33 city blocks. Two years later they partnered with A.C. Daley and added 24 more blocks that became the Daley Addition.

1874 Richland City, Buena Vista Township, Richland County, Wisconsin

Each block consisted of eight building lots 66 feet wide, 132 feet deep, and streets 66 feet wide. Four streets— Water, Front, Washington, and Railroad Streets—ran parallel with the river. North and south cross streets were Hill, Oak, Grove, Fulton, Court, Franklin, and Pine.

People came; building lots were purchased and Richland City soon began to flourish. By the fall of 1849 there were twelve buildings; businessmen and craftsmen recognized the great potential of this embryo village and started establishing their places of commerce. Ezekiel McIntyre opened the first store in a log cabin, soon followed by cobbler, Henry Clayman; tailor, Henry Dillon; another tailor, John Wyker; wagon builder, Samuel Tyler; cabinetmaker, Chester Goodwin from Maine; carpenter, New York native Daniel Nichols; blacksmith, Peter Kaskins; General Store, Daniel Osborn; jeweler, German watchmaker Christian Spidel; physician, Dr. Hartshorn; Dr. G.W. Hadder established the first dental practice; and ferry service between Richland City and Sand Prairie (destined to become Avoca) on the south bank of the Wisconsin River was established and run for eight years by Daniel Nichols. (In 1862 Daniel Nichols enlisted in the 19th Regiment Wisconsin Volunteer Infantry. He had served eleven months when he was discharged for disability. He re-enlisted a year later in the 4th Wisconsin Battery, light artillery, in which he served until the close of the Civil War.)

People built homes, and soon there were three churches— Methodist, Presbyterian, and Congregational. A post office was established in 1854 with John Rutan as the first postmaster.

Flourmills were a common sight in many pioneer towns; a steam grist and flouring mill was erected in 1854 by Henry Rowell. This mill contained four run of stones; its machinery was installed by George Sargent, one of the early engineers on the upper Mississippi and its navigable branches from 1845 to 1875. Rowell owned the mill for about a year, and then it went into the hands of other owners, continuing to be quite successful for a number of years. But it proved to be of too great magnitude to be profitable in this location, and was eventually dismantled and moved to Milwaukee.

Ephraim Brown erected Richland City's first sawmill in 1855. Soon afterward, William Ketchum bought half interest. This steam powered mill did an extensive business producing lumber not only from logs that were floated down the river from northern pineries, but even sawed and finished the oak, maple, and black walnut hardwoods that grew abundantly in the county. Brown and Ketchum ran the mill for a number of years, then sold it to new owners, and its use was finally discontinued in 1870.

Colonel Hugo Bock established a distillery at Richland City in 1869. (His title was a term of respect, not a military rank, although he did serve as a private in the 3rd Alabama Infantry.) A native of New York, he went to New Orleans as a young man where he eventually was put in charge of a distillery there and learned the trade. At Richland City, his business included wholesale dealing in foreign and domestic liquors and wines, as well as those produced in his own facility. A most popular item was his fine wine made from common wild grapes, favorably compared with the very best California varieties. He also bred specialty race horses and maintained an oval racetrack at Richland City.

Bock house as it appears today at its Gotham location.
(Photo by Dan Bomkamp)

Bock built an elegant home at Richland City in 1878, of classic Italianate design, typical of a southern mansion. But because of the severe erosion of the Wisconsin River banks, the house was moved ¾ mile to its present location in Gotham in 1908, where it remains a current residence.

A schoolhouse was erected in 1853 and soon after that an academy that allowed youth to earn the equivalent of a high school education. The next year, 1854, Wallace and Greene sold a lot to the School District for the sum of one dollar. The structure erected was quite inadequate by modern standards; only the most rugged students could endure the cold during the winter months. Although this "academy" did not last long, it gave Richland City the distinction of having a school of higher learning, which included teacher training and preparation for other professions.

To accommodate Richland City's rapid growth, Jacob Coffinberry platted an additional sixty-four blocks adjacent to the east end of Richland City, doubling the size of the little town. Streets parallel to the Wisconsin River were extended into the new addition, and Madison and University Streets were added; Market Street was added to the riverfront. North and south cross streets— Taylor, Columbus, Ewing, Pearl, Upper Ferry, Jefferson, and Adams were created in the new addition.

Richland City had become the most important regular freight and passenger port for the Wisconsin River boat traffic between Portage and Prairie du Chien, and with the influx of more businesses and population growth, the new town was quickly becoming the region's busiest center of commerce. In addition to the goods and services sold in the river port town, nearly all goods destined for the rest of Richland County arrived via the river steamboats and passed through Richland City.

Lumber raft on the Wisconsin River

Riverboat crews frequently spent nights in Richland City, and with a steady increase in travelers arriving via the boats, not only did the stores and shops enjoy a thriving business; lodging became an important necessity. Three hotels were established beginning in 1853: the Bangham Tavern (burned to the ground and was replaced in 1856 by the Valley House), Jacob Hauxhurst, proprietor; the Union House, Jacob Coffinberry, proprietor; and the City Hotel, J.W. Frame, proprietor.

Union House,
AT RICHLAND CITY,
BY C. BRE,

RULES.
No Liquor allowed to be drank in or about the House.
No gambling or card playing allowed.
No profane, obscene, or vulgar language allowed.
No one allowed to remain who is intoxicated.
No sky-larking allowed.

RATES OF FARE.
Meals, each,   37½
Lodging, one night,   25
Board by the week, with lodging, $3 00
Board by the week, without lodging,   2 50
Board by the day, with lodging,   1 00

STABLE RATES.
Horse to hay over night,   25
Horse to hay and grain over night,   37½
Horse to hay, grain and care over night,   50
April 28, 1856.   [24]

Richland City was not without its share of rowdiness, typical of most river towns. Brawls were common among the river crews after spending time at *Snow and Eddy's*, a popular gathering place for the rivermen, as well as the local male population, to spend their leisure time. A need for an authority figure to keep the peace was obvious; William Lewis arrived from Indiana in 1856 to become the first Justice of the Peace, an office he held for 22 years.

A sound and healthy business atmosphere certainly contributed to the prosperity of Richland City. Its one major drawback, however, was the lack of roads leading to it. The water route was still the primary mode of travel, but the Wisconsin River's water levels were inconsistent during the summer months, causing difficult or totally suspended navigation much of the time.

County officials recognized the importance of roads for improving commerce and growth. Lack of a good road had already spurred the moving of the county seat from Orion to Richland Center, another rapidly advancing community, but with overland routes to other towns and the newly established State Capital, Madison. Appropriations were made, and a road was built from Richland City along the Pine River to the mouth of Ash Creek. This improved the condition, but it wasn't the total solution to the problem. More change was on the horizon.

Railroads were on the rise to becoming an important transportation factor; the Milwaukee/Prairie du Chien Railroad was eager to extend its railway to the Mississippi River. A survey was well underway along the Wisconsin River valley that would place the tracks on the north side of the river, passing through Richland City; however, a few landowners thought they could hold out for a lot more money than the railroad company was offering. Adding to the dilemma, a highly opinionated resident at Richland City was not shy to express her views regarding the rumor claiming that the railway was to pass right through her house; she protested quite vigorously. But trying to bully the railroad company with high land prices and protests backfired.

To avoid the exorbitant land prices and legal battles with the opposing resident, railroad officials chose to bridge the Wisconsin at Lone Rock and construct their line on the more receptive south side of the river passing through Avoca and Muscoda. This decision to bypass Richland City was, perhaps, the beginning of the end for the town.

The railroads offered faster and more efficient freight and passenger transportation than riverboats relying on water levels of the undependable Wisconsin River. Once the railroad was in operation, steamboat traffic stopped and Richland City's vigorous commerce came to a grinding halt. Goods were shipped by rail to other points of distribution, and the booming business of the little town was no more. Shortsighted attitudes of a few people had started the death march. Over the next ten years, the abrupt decline caused businesses to close; people moved out of the town. Failure to attract the railroad had brought on its demise.

Despite all the drastic changes, the village held on for a few more years. Then, in 1866 General Jonathan Moore, an army officer and resident of Muscoda, a village ten miles downriver from Richland City, built a bridge across the Wisconsin. The 1,712 feet long bridge connected Richland, Grant, and Iowa Counties, and with the already present railroad, Muscoda became an important shipping point for grain and livestock.

The bridge was yet another negative factor in Richland City's future, but the final blow came, not from competing towns, not from other means of travel, but from Mother Nature, when the channel of the Wisconsin River changed and the full force of the current began eating away at the soft soil where Richland City was built.

Some people claimed that this change in the river channel was the fault of Ed Wallace who was given the contract to build wing dams at Point Independence, a little upriver from Richland City. These wing dams which were piles of rocks extending out from the shore toward the middle of the river were put in place to keep Avoca from flooding. Wallace hired farmers for miles around who came with a hundred wagon teams to haul rocks for the wing dam construction. Whether these wing dams changed the channel enough, or nature just did what happens normally, the channel began moving north; Richland City was right in its path. At normal stage, the current delivers 100,000 gallons of water per second down the valley. That means millions of gallons of water per day washed away sand and mud, and in time, the riverbanks at Richland City began collapsing into the river.

Long before the glaciers melted and Glacial Lake Wisconsin broke through the barrier containing it, the ancient Wisconsin River was there. The upper river runs along miles of channels cut into bedrock. The lower sections of the river are different. Here the river is bordered on one side or the other by large expanses of marshes, soft ground covered with saw grass, ponds and swampland. Here, the river can change its course as it cuts away these sand banks and marshes, as opposed to the upper river that is held in place by virtue of the bedrock channels.

Water from springs and rain runoff from the hills naturally flow downhill to the bottoms of valleys where it accumulates and forms streams, and then continues its downhill flow through the valley as the terrain slopes; the greater the slope, the faster the current. In the case of the Wisconsin River, the elevation at Lone Rock is 709 feet above sea level. The elevation at Muscoda is 680 feet above sea level, meaning that the river drops 29 feet in the 15 miles it travels through this area. That is about two feet of drop in every mile of river resulting in a very fast current. But the rate of drop isn't constant along the entire river; in some places it may drop several feet in a mile while in others it is nearly flat, dropping only a few inches. In those areas with greater drop, the current is naturally faster. In addition to the speed, another factor exerts influence on the river current's motion. The earth's rotation is constant, and even though it is unnoticeable when observed from a riverbank, the earth's spinning causes the water to swirl like a giant corkscrew as it flows.

Most waterways meander back and forth across the valley containing them due to this motion. Where it comes against a soft bank, the corkscrew action of the water cuts into the bank and washes it away, causing a bend in the stream. By the same process, the Wisconsin River also meanders down the valley. Viewing the river from a high bluff or an airplane, it is surprising how crooked the river channel really is. And it was this process that was coming into play at Richland City, in addition to the influence of the wing dams.

One more factor can be considered: thousands of years ago the Pine River and its tributaries were hundreds of times larger than they are now, as was the Wisconsin River equally larger. The delta that was formed (as described in previous chapters) at the confluence of the two rivers was actually protected from erosion by the then stronger current of the Pine River, pushing the Wisconsin's current away from its banks. But as the Pine lost its volume and the current slowed, the Wisconsin's channel moved northward toward the delta because of the reduced resistance. At the Richland City delta, there is no bedrock containing the Wisconsin, unlike upriver at Lone Rock where there is solid rock keeping the channel in check, and below Richland City, bedrock on the north side of the river extends nearly all the way to Muscoda. There was nothing to stop the current from moving against the delta made up of only sand, clay and mud, and in the early 1860s the soft riverbank at Richland City slowly began to "melt" into the river.

Choice riverfront lots simply vanished over time, and then Water Street disappeared. Slowly but steadily the next tier of blocks and Front Street slid into the water. With every spring flood or heavy rainfall causing a rise of the Wisconsin, a little more of Richland City was swept away; its fate was sealed.

Gotham

Appearance of original Gotham Railroad Depot has fortunately retained its historic appeal.
It is now a residence. (Photo by Dan Bomkamp)

A narrow gauge railroad spur was built in 1876 from Lone Rock to Richland Center that passed ¾ mile north of Richland City. As was the case with many towns of that time period, when the railroad line did not pass within the city limits, people panicked, believing their town was doomed. Richland City had been bypassed once before, and now it was apparent that the fate of the town was darkening even more.

William McNurlen laid out a new town to the north, built a depot and handled the freight coming into and leaving the area. The Bock distillery and blending plant was still operating, and it produced a considerable amount of freight. For a while many of the old timers wanted to keep the name Richland City, but by then, Richland Center had become the county seat, and there was often confusion with mail and freight being delivered to the wrong town. The Railroad impatiently requested that the town be given a name, suggesting *McNurlen*. The founder, William McNurlen, was not in favor of such a name; there had already been confusion with similar town names, and there already existed another Wisconsin town with a similar name—McFarland. Instead, he chose his sea captain friend's name, *Gotham*.

The man for whom the new town was named, Myron Wheeler Gotham, was born in New York and had spent his life since the age of eighteen on boats on the Great Lakes. He and his wife settled on a farm on the banks of the Pine River near Richland City in 1867. They raised a family of eight children. Gotham spent his winters in Richland County and was the captain of the *Silvanus J. Macy* during the navigational season.

Captain Myron Wheeler Gotham

Sylvanus J. Macy

The *Macy* left Buffalo, New York on November 28, 1902 with her consort, the barge *Mable Wilson,* both carrying coal. Two of Gotham's sons, Lucius, age 18 and Myron, age 24 were among the crew onboard the *Macy,* and Gotham's brother, J.E. Gotham, captained the *Wilson.*

It was near the end of the Great Lakes shipping season; by the time the *Macy* and *Wilson* had crossed to the north side of Lake Erie, the weather had worsened to the point of casting off the *Wilson's* tow lines, naturally causing great concern as the two vessels separated. As the *Macy* moved through the storm off Point Burwell seeking a sheltering port, it suddenly vanished from sight. The *Wilson's* captain could do nothing more than watch as his brother and nephews went to the bottom of the lake. The *Wilson* reached safety the next day with news of the disaster.

The bodies of Captain Gotham and his son, Lucius, were recovered and buried at their home in Richland County. The body of the other son, Myron, was found later in Canadian waters and returned home.

Captain Myron Gotham's house as it appears today in the Village of Gotham. (Photo by Dan Bomkamp)

Paul Seifert's Richland City home and taxidermy shop that were moved to Gotham in 1908 when they were threatened by deteriorating Wisconsin River banks.

Paul Seifert's home on the Bennett farm where he last lived and died in 1921.

Originally built as an opera house, this structure eventually became Gotham's City Hall.

Gotham street scene approx. 1915-1920

Paul Seifert's home in Gotham as it appears today. (Photo by Dan Bomkamp)

Other Buildings Moved from Richland City to Lone Rock
(Photos by Dan Bomkamp)

Blacksmith Shop

Dillon's Tailor Shop

Private Residence

The Young Paul Seifert

School graduation photograph, 1867

When researching the early life of Paul Seifert, writers have portrayed many different versions of his life before he arrived in Richland City. Much of the information has been derived from the letter from *Baron von Wolfgang.* Paul Seifert translated this letter to English; it was delivered after his death by Indian relic collector E.F. Richter to Charles Brown of the Wisconsin Historical Society. It would seem that many writers have taken the information in this letter as truth, when, in reality, it seems that it is far from the truth. Sometimes, disproving the falsehoods is as important as proving the facts.

Dr. Adolph Seifert (Paul's father)

Ernestina Augusta Schmorl (Paul's mother)
and Paul Adolph Seifert

Facts vs. Fiction

Paul Seifert was born June 11, 1846 in Dresden, Germany. The Wolfgang letter tells us that Paul's parents were aristocrats and his father, Dr. Adolph Seifert, was a university professor. This information is not completely accurate.

A researcher in Germany, Jutta Wiese, reports that Paul's father, Dr. Johann Gottfried Adolf Seifert, was a teacher at *Freimaureeinstitut,* or *Freemason's Institute,* and that he was of the lower middle class. His mother's name was Johanne Ernestine Seifert. Their address was the same as the school's, among a list of several teachers who worked there. This suggests that they lived in housing furnished by the school with many other teachers, and indicates that Paul Seifert's parents were not aristocrats. Paul is said to have learned taxidermy from the groundskeeper employed by his father, but if the family lived at the school in furnished housing, it is doubtful that his father employed a gardener. It is possible that there was a gardener and he may have taught Paul taxidermy, but he was probably not the Seifert family's employee.

The Wolfgang letter tells that Paul and his brother enrolled in the University at Leipzig in the spring of 1865. Research has shown that Paul enrolled at *Forstakademie* or School of Forestry in Tharandt where he attended classes in 1866 and 1867. He did not attend Leipzig University.

The threat of war was in the air in the spring of 1866. The conflict was between the Germans under leadership of the Austrian Empire, and the Kingdom of Prussia with its German allies and Italy. The Prussian army of 225,000 soldiers possessed a distinct advantage with its far superior weaponry than that of the German soldiers consisting of 240,000 Austrians and 25,000 Saxons.

The war began on June 14, 1866; on July 3, the battle of Sadowa became the decisive battle of the war. When it was over, the Prussians had suffered less than two thousand dead and just over seven thousand wounded. The Germans, however, sustained much greater losses: 5,793 dead, 8,514 wounded, 7,836 missing, and 9,291 captured. (If we are to believe von Wolfgang's letter, he was one of the wounded, Paul's brother, Joseph, was one of the dead, and Paul was one of the prisoners. Yet records indicate that Paul didn't have a brother, and at the time of this war, Paul was still in school.)

New laws enacted in July of 1867 declared that the Kingdom of Saxony (Paul's homeland) no longer existed. With his home under rule of the Prussians, there was nothing to keep young Paul from leaving Germany. In mid-September 1867, just ten weeks after graduation from the Forestry Academy, Paul sailed on the ship *Eugenie* from Hamburg destined for the United States.

Ship Eugenie 1889

At age 21 Paul Seifert arrived in New York on November 2, 1867. Records show that he was listed as being a farmer, but all questions regarding what he planned to do or where he would go in the United States were answered "Unknown." It is possible that his lack of English language skills prevented him from answering any differently. However, he wasted little time getting to Wisconsin, as later in his life, he wrote about how things were in Richland City when he *arrived in 1867.*

Paul Comes To Richland City

How did a 21-year-old man who had landed in New York City with very little money, nowhere to live, and having little knowledge of the American culture find his way to Richland City in Wisconsin? Was there a reason he chose this place or was it just chance? Somehow he chose Wisconsin as his destination and made his way to Madison. From there he traveled to Portage where he boarded a flatboat headed down the Wisconsin River.

Only a speculative possibility exists that Paul may have known of Henry (Heinrich) Seifert living in nearby Dayton Township. (Henry was born in Germany and had lived in Wisconsin since the late 1840s; however, research indicates that there was no family connection.) The easiest access to Dayton Township at that time would have been up the Pine River, which might explain—with little certainty—why he landed at Richland City.

It is also possible—but not certain—that Paul's family

knew the Lorenzo Kraft family in Germany. Lorenzo Kraft was born in Baden in 1801. By the time Paul arrived at Richland City, the Kraft family was well established there, owning three adjacent lots. The family spoke fluent English as well as German,

Paul's family tells the story that Lorenzo Kraft's daughter, Elizabeth, was on the bank one day watching a flatboat as it rode the current down the river. She was very surprised to see a young man jump off the boat and swim to shore. She later commented, "He looked like a drowned rat." That drowned rat was Paul Seifert.

Did Paul leap off the boat and swim to shore? Did he even know that he was at Richland City? We'll probably never know those answers for sure, but Paul *did* arrive, and this is where his story in America really begins.

Author's note: Considering the time required to process as an immigrant upon arriving in New York, and then traveling to Madison, Wisconsin, then to Portage, then down the Wisconsin River on a flatboat, Paul's arrival at Richland City would have been—at the earliest—late November or early December. Considering air and water temperatures at that time of year, it seems highly unlikely that this actually happened. J.L.F.

When Paul arrived at Richland City he had little money, and his experience with American culture was minimal. Lorenzo Kraft and his family spoke German, and perhaps, because of Elizabeth Kraft, Paul was drawn to them. They took him in and helped him get started in this new place. For a short time Paul lived in a small house next door to the Krafts. It is not known who owned the house, but surely the Kraft family was instrumental in arranging the accommodations.

During that time Paul courted Elizabeth. On October 9, 1868 they married, and their first two daughters, Ernestina and Lena May were born in the following two years.

Elizabeth Seifert purchased twenty acres of land In October 1871just a short distance east of Bogus Bluff in Buena Vista Township. There, Paul and Elizabeth started their homestead, making their living by gardening and selling vegetables and flowers to area residents. Their gardens were showplaces, and Paul was known to push a wheelbarrow into town several times a day to sell his vegetables. To supplement their livelihood, Paul hunted and fished and worked at taxidermy. He made friends and traded with the local Indians. (Seifert reported to Charles Brown "that in 1867 and after as many as 500 Winnebago Indians camped in the Pine River Valley near Richland City. Old Mike and White Otter were chiefs.") Elizabeth sewed for the local residents and area Indians, and she sold her hand-woven baskets.

Their third and fourth daughters, Elizabeth and Bertha were born in1876 and1880.

Elizabeth bought an additional forty acres of land that lay next to their farm in January of 1881. During the summer months they continued extensive gardening and sold produce to make money for the household. But Paul had also become a very successful collector of Indian artifacts and sold many to other private collectors. It was during this time that Paul became acquainted with E.H. Stiles who owned land in Richland City and raised and sold fruit.

Elijah H. Stiles moved to Richland City from Waterloo, Wisconsin in 1888. He was born in 1831 in Jefferson County near Aztalan, and as a young man he became a student under Milwaukee Museum's archeologist, Charles E. Brown. Stiles' contribution to the Milwaukee Museum consisting of artifacts he found in Jefferson County was of such great proportion that it warranted the expansion of the museum eightfold in 1894.

Mr. Stiles was not pleased with Paul selling artifacts, and he eventually convinced Paul that the relics should be studied and placed in museums rather than being scattered across the country in private collections. He introduced Paul to Charles Brown—then associated with the Wisconsin State Historical Society. They became great friends. Brown, too, impressed upon Paul the need to preserve the artifacts that he found and to pass them on to coming generations. Paul then began donating specimens to museums.

Paul found hundreds if not thousands of artifacts during his lifetime. That could easily convince a person of today to believe that he must have found a place full of wonderful ancient relics, and that the Indian Burial Cave really existed. It doesn't seem likely that he could just casually search the hills and valleys and find as many things as he donated and sold.

Further research about the area—Richland City in particular—tends to shed a different light on the sources of his collection. It seems obvious, now, that the bulk of the artifacts Paul found were from the ancient mounds along the Wisconsin River bank, easily recovered by sifting through the sand as the shoreline gradually deteriorated and fell away from solid land. Six thousand years' worth of buried artifacts suddenly were exposed, and there for easy picking.

No one paid much attention to a piece of the riverbank that fell into the Wisconsin River now and then. When spring floods rose, large sections of the sandy banks often fell into the water and were carried away. By 1874 there was some loss of land, but all of the Richland City lots were still intact and no one displayed any concern.

It was during that time that Ed Wallace was given the task of building his wing dam upriver from Richland City; the purpose of the wing dam was to help prevent flooding of Avoca, the village near the southern bank. No one can be certain if that caused the river channel to move north, but it probably contributed to the end result. Whatever the reason, the riverbank at Richland City began caving away and there was nothing anyone could do to stop it.

It was said that at times huge sections fell at once causing a loud booming sound. By 1895 Front Street and River Street were gone, taking 16 blocks and about 90 building lots with them. When it was laid out in 1849, Richland City, was approximately 1,800 feet from north to south. The first 800 feet facing the river was gone by the late 1890s; by 1919 another 600 feet of Richland City real estate had dropped into the river. Many homes were moved; some by loading them onto barges and floating them down the river to other locations, and some were moved to Lone Rock by rolling them on logs with teams of horses. There was little left of the once thriving village.

Even more convincing of Paul's source of ancient relics is a map that Paul made for Charles Brown, locating over sixty mounds on the Richland City site. Some, but not all, were burial mounds; bones and sometimes entire skeletons accompanied by hundreds of historical remnants were often exposed as the mounds crashed down onto the river shoreline.

Once Paul began finding these artifacts he surely kept an eye on the river, carefully watching for rising water. He had mapped the mounds, so he was quite familiar with their locations, and he recognized when one was threatened by the collapsing bank. The booming sounds made by the falling banks alerted Paul and Elizabeth to scavenge the loosened soil for new treasures. In theory, the land where Richland City was built had been inhabited for over 6,000 years by several different cultures, so it is a logical conclusion that there would be

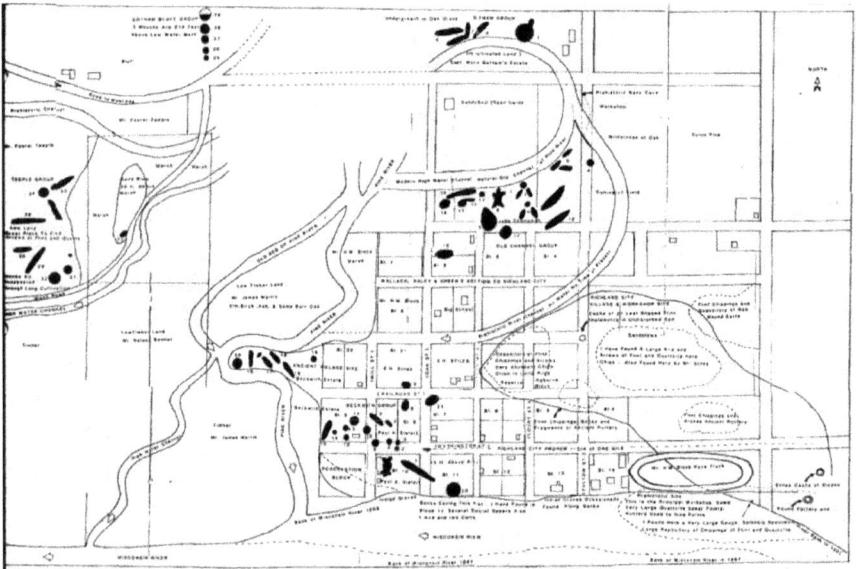

A MAP OF THE RICHLAND CITY VILLAGE AND WORKSHOP SITE, BUENA VISTA TOWNSHIP, RICHLAND COUNTY, WISCONSIN PREPARED BY PAUL A. SEIFERT & ELIJAH H. STILES IN 1903

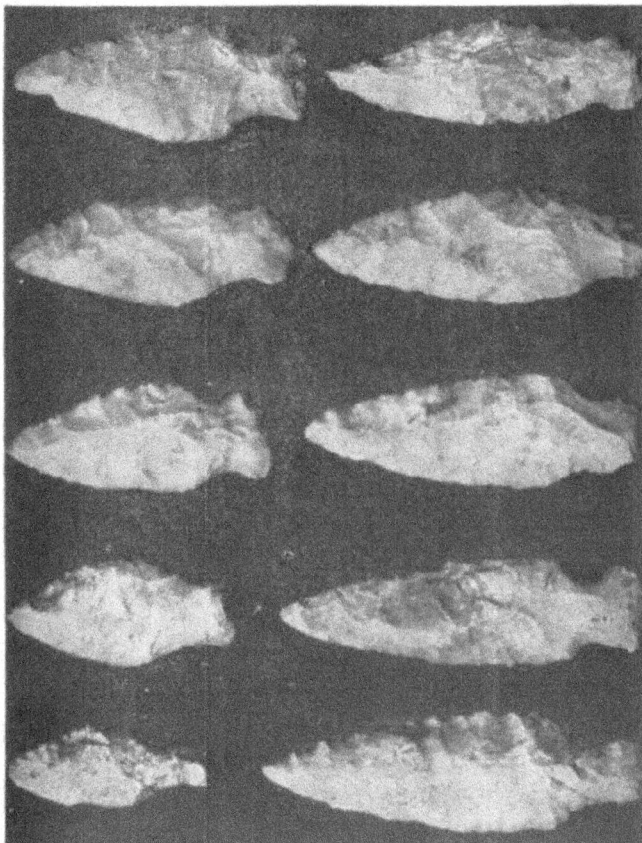

Flint arrowpoints found at Richland City

arrowheads, spear points, tools and more left behind by the people who lived there. Seifert obviously had a good eye for such things, and he knew when to be there at the right time to harvest the riches.

This is not to say the Indian Burial Cave does not exist, however, the crumbling riverbank seems more plausible. Paul was quite popular among the riverboat crews, frequently entertaining them as a "teller of tall tales," and his story of a burial cave certainly fits that description.

Real
or Hoax?

Where did Paul uncover these treasures? If the Wolfgang letter is believed to be reliable, he located a cave full of Indian skeletons and a vast treasure trove of spear points, arrowheads and other wonderful specimens. The cave is described in Wolfgang's letter, but there are too many questionable issues about that letter that reduce the probability of it containing a totally true and accurate story. Likewise, it is questionable that Von Wolfgang was a real person; he and the contents of the letter could be products of imagination.

Several things about the letter tend to discredit its validity:

1. Paul Seifert did not have a brother.
2. Paul Seifert did not attend Leipzig University.
3. The letter was supposedly published in the *Vienna Courier*, but that newspaper did not exist at the time of the claimed publication. It came much later.
4. Thousands of passenger lists of ships arriving in New York were searched, and not one included a passenger with the name of *Wolfgang.*
5. The name *Wolfgang* is almost never used as a surname, but is rather common as a first name.
6. If the writing style in the Wolfgang letter is compared to Paul's letters to Charles Brown, it is easy to see that they were not written by the same person. The language in the Wolfgang letter is much more polished and elegant. The writer was well educated and fluent in English. For example, the writer of the Wolfgang letter says:

    > *In the Spring of 1887 one morning I received like always my mail from the postman. Amongst my letters was one post stamp Richland City, Wisconsin, North America. Judge my surprise, who could know me in that far off Country? I opened the letter and it was from Paul.*

Paul's letters were crude and often full of grammatical errors. He always got right to the point and didn't bother with extra description. An excerpt from letters to Charles Brown written by Paul typically read:

> *Last week I found an interesting find. My wife and me went on the sand East of the vil-*

*lage. We found a place of stones like this un-
covered from the sand. We dig in the middle
about 2 feet deep.*

*Researcher note: The Wisconsin Historical Society has twenty-
four letters written by Paul Seifert to Charles E. Brown. These
letters are vital to understanding the relationship between these
men. Too extensive to be included in this book, they are accessi-
ble in the WHS archives. R.N.*

Paul was known to tell a tall tale now and then but if the above excerpts are compared, it is easily detected that Paul did not compose the Wolfgang letter himself, even though the translation is in Paul's handwriting. The person who wrote the original in German certainly knew a lot about Paul and the area. He knew where Paul lived and that Bogus Bluff was downriver from his home; he knew the towns visible from atop the hill, namely Avoca, Muscoda and Lone Rock; he knew the railway station was in Gotham and not in Richland City; he writes of various ancient sites in the area, which is accurate.

So who was this mysterious writer of the *Rose Colored Spear letter?* Is it a hoax? Why would Paul Seifert go to the extremes to create a fictional story and a false friend—Von Wolfgang—and then have the translation of a fake letter delivered to his good friend, Charles Brown after his own death? If the Burial Cave really existed, why didn't Paul show it to Brown while he was still alive? It will probably never be known for certain. There are no good answers to these questions.

But we can certainly speculate with some *possible* answers. No doubt, Paul Seifert was made aware of the Big Eagle Cave legend, perhaps from the local Native Americans that he be-friended and with whom he continued trade relations. Paul saw an opportunity.

It may be doubtful that Paul ever actually entered such a cave, as his daughter stated (after his death) that she was con-vinced the cave story was manufactured. Paul had been sur-rounded by many people who were fluent in German and Eng-lish, and he could have enlisted one of them to compose the *Rose Colored Spear* letter in a more elegant fashion than he was capable of himself.

Why did he keep the letter from falling into the hands of his friend, Charles Brown at the Wisconsin Historical Society until after his death? Brown would have had an intense inter-est in such a cave for the historical value it contained. If the story was imagined, the delay prevented Mr. Brown from re-questing Seifert to escort him to the cave.

Was this Seifert's attempt at fame? It is quite ironic that he had already made that mark... he just didn't know it. His farm scene paintings (discussed in the next chapter) would propel him to a high level of notoriety in years to come.

Paul Seifert, the Painter

Paul Seifert was a man of talent. Although he earned his livelihood mainly from the flowers and vegetables that he grew and sold, and dabbled in taxidermy for supplemental income, he developed a knack for selling the artifacts he found, both in the United States and abroad, for 35 years.

But he cultivated another talent—one that he learned at the German school—that would propel his significance into the Twenty-first century. The folk art farm scenes that he began painting in the late 1870s are considered quite valuable today, however, Paul was paid as little as $2.50 to $3.00 for each image by the farm owner. He traveled to the farms, negotiated a deal, and then went to work; sometimes he sketched the farm and returned to his workshop to make the painting. Other times he would stay right at the farm and work on the painting until it was finished.

The vast majority of his paintings are one of a kind. There were a few instances when the farmer wanted more than one copy made. The late Frank Shadewald had one such example of a painting of his grandfather's farm which was one of six. Frank's painting is one of the first made and is very precise and typical of Paul's work. The later copies became less and less exact and weren't of Paul's usual quality, probably because boredom befell him from doing the same thing over and over.

Paul liked order in his life and it was obvious in his paintings. His lines were straight and almost like technical drawings made by an architect. He often added people and animals to the scenes. He did most of his paintings in watercolors on cardboard. It is not known for sure how many of these he made; most were not signed, or the signature was cut off along with the name of the farm.

His artistry is not limited to watercolors; he also painted on glass using oil paint. These were of castles in Germany that he drew from his memory. He sketched the picture on a board and then laid a pane of glass over it, and painted the scene on the glass. He even used silver and gold foil on the paintings to make windows appear as light was coming from them. Few of these paintings exist, but they are exceptionally beautiful.

It is for his artful renderings that Paul has become known as one of the most important Primitive Painters in America. He is often compared to Grandma Moses, another Primitive Painter who came after Paul, and achieved much success and notoriety during her lifetime. They both painted scenes that are similar in style, yet much different in content.

Many of Paul Seifert's watercolor farm scenes, as well as the few oil paintings on glass, grace the walls of various museums and are considered nearly priceless. Occasionally, someone comes across one in an attic and puts it up for auction. One was found in 1991 that sold for $19,000. Another in 1996 sold for $13,000 and one in 1998 sold for $24,000. One lucky person found one recently that sold for $66,000.

Paul Seifert led an incredible life. He came to the new world from a far away country, and made a lasting name for himself. While he lived he had no idea that his paintings would someday hang in museums and homes, and that a single painting would be worth more than he earned in his entire lifetime.

He loved his home and family and was known as an entertaining, clever man who liked a little of the spirits now and then. Many times, while reading articles about him, the term "generous to a fault" was used to describe Paul; he was always ready to help someone in need.

During an age when a human life was relatively short as compared to present day, Paul lived a long life of 75 years. Most that pass through this life are gone and forgotten, but Paul lives on in his paintings and his stories, and the legend of the Indian Burial Cave.

Paul and Elizabeth in their garden.

Mr. and Mrs. Paul Seifert on the bank of the Wisconsin River

Not much remains of Paul and Elizabeth Seifert's homestead. All that is left is a grassy field and a stone foundation of a springhouse on the hillside. Imagine how it appeared when they lived there; imagine Paul pushing his wheelbarrow down the road to sell his vegetables.

(Photo by Dan Bomkamp)

Paul Seifert and his wife Elizabeth are buried in Button Cemetery,
located just east of Gotham on County Road JJ.
(Photo by Ron Nagel)

Richland City Today

If you didn't know the story of Richland City, you would view the last few remaining hundred feet of land, and have no idea that a thriving community once stood there. A short way south on Fulton Street from Hwy 60 in the Village of Gotham is found the area once filled with streets, homes, businesses, churches, and a school, all that were once a vibrant part of so many lives. The river now occupies the space where most of the village once stood, with its present south bank where the north bank was when Richland City thrived.

The Bock house that once stood on the riverbank has been moved into Gotham and is still an occupied home. Bock's carriage house was converted to a residence, but has since burned down. The home of Captain Myron Gotham still stands in the southern part of the Village of Gotham near the northern boundary of Richland City.

The riverbank at Richland City continues to be eroded by the never-ending current of the Wisconsin River. Each spring, high water eats away more and more of the supporting sand, and chunks of topsoil and vegetation are swallowed up by the river. Perhaps in a few hundred years it may be knocking on the door of the Village of Gotham.

Satellite view of Richland City today (Google Maps)

Place of Enchantment

The Wisconsin River as viewed from atop Bogus Bluff.
(Photo by Ron Nagel)

This ancient river valley has been here for thousands of years and will doubtless be here thousands of years after we are all gone. Many lives existed in this valley, from the ancient people who were here before the pyramids, to the people of today with their ever-increasing technology. It is sincerely hoped that the stories and legends will be passed down to future generations, and that they will be just as enthralled with the epic history of the River of Mystery.

References and Sources:

Books

Young America – A Folk Art History; The Flowering of American Folk Art; American Folk Painters of Three Centuries; Paths of the mound building Indians and great game Animals; The Antiques of Wisconsin as examined and surveyed; Primitive Painters in America 1750-1950; The Wisconsin River – An Odyssey Through Space and Time; History of Richland County 1906; The History of Crawford and Richland County Wisconsin 1889; The Wisconsin Blue Book; Wisconsin State Gazetteer; Counterfeiting in America; Counterfeiting in Colonial America; True Detective Stories; Richland Center Wisconsin, A History; Antiquities of Wisconsin.

Magazines

Wisconsin Trails; The Wisconsin Archeologist; The Wisconsin Speleologist; Wisconsin Magazine; Wisconsin Magazine of History; Lost Treasure Magazine.

Newspapers

Wisconsin State Journal; Richland Democrat; Muscoda Progressive; The Richland County Republican; Richland Rustic; The Weekly Wisconsin; The Republican Observer; The Capital Times; The Milwaukee Journal; The Daily Northwestern; La Crosse Tribune; The Milwaukee Sentinel; The Avoca Headlight; Crawford County Courier; Appleton Post Crescent.

Archives

Richland County History Room; Dresden Archives – Dresden Germany; State of Wisconsin Historical Society- Charles E. Brown papers; State of Wisconsin Historical Society- Wisconsin Archeological Society Records; Lower Wisconsin River Genealogical and Historical Research Center; Iowa County Historical Society; Technical University of Dresden archives; Wisconsin Geological Museum; Leipzig University archives – Leipzig, Germany.

Papers

Geographical and Natural History Survey – List of Wisconsin Caves; The Tragedy of Richland City; Pine River Site survey for WI DOT; Transactions of the Wisconsin Academy of Sciences, Arts, and Letters; The Journal of Capt. Henry Whiting – 1819; American Fur Company papers; The diary of Simon Augustus Sherman 1849-1850.

Web Sites

Ancestry.com; Madison.com; Wisconsinhistory.org; freimaurer-wiki.de; Castlegarden.org.

About The Authors

Dan Bomkamp has made his home in the Wisconsin River valley all his life with the exception of his college years in La Crosse. He has been an avid hunter and fisherman his whole life. For many years he was in the sporting goods industry and began writing in the 80s for outdoor magazines. He is active in the Foreign Exchange Student program having hosted 33 boys from 13 countries over the years. Golden Retrievers have also been a big part of his life. He had at least one Golden sharing his home for 33 years. He lives in Muscoda with his cat, Tigger and his Boston Terrier, Buster.

J.L. Fredrick lived his youth in rural Western Wisconsin not far from the Mississippi River. He attended a one-room country school for his first seven years of education. Wisconsin has been home most of his life. After college in La Crosse, Wisconsin and a stint with Uncle Sam during the Viet Nam era, the next few years he explored and experimented with life's options. He entered into the transportation industry in 1975 where he remained until retirement in 2012. He is a long-time member of the Wisconsin State Historical Society. Author of sixteen novels and non-fiction history volumes, he was a featured author during Grand Excursion 2004.

J.L. Fredrick currently resides at Poynette, Wisconsin.

Ron Nagel grew up covered with poison ivy. Eventually, his parents moved to town in an attempt to keep him out of the woods. It's not surprising that he took on this adventure to locate a lost cave.

With a degree in electronics, Ron spent 20+ years in the computer industry. By applying logical thinking, and patience, most any computer problem can be solved. The same could be said about lost caves. He has been on a 35-year-long odyssey searching for a cave that he is certain is there.

Ron Nagel lives in Verona, Wisconsin. He enjoys old things, so you will find him often in antique shops. He is currently planning a 2014 Wyoming adventure seeking an explanation to a strange rock formation he discovered by scrutinizing details on a satellite map while researching a lost gold mine. His complete 35 years of Seifert and Bogus Bluff research will eventually be posted on:

www.CaveOfTheDead.com.

Other titles available from Lovstad Publishing:

By J.L. Fredrick

Rivers, Roads, & Rails
Thunder in the Night
Cursed by the Wind
Another Shade of Gray
The Gaslight Knights
September Ten
The Great Train Robbery of Monroe County
Aftermath
The Other End of the Tunnel
Mad City Bust
Dance With a Tornado
Across the Dead Line
Across the Second Dead Line
The Private Journal of Clancy Crane
Unfinished Business
As I Recall...

www.JLFredrick.com   www.Lovstadpublishing.com

Other titles available from Lovstad Publishing:

By Dan Bomkamp

The Adventures of Thunderfoot
More Adventures of Thunderfoot
Thanks, Thunderfoot
The Gosey
Big Edna
Lost Flight
Voyageur
Tag
Spirit
Whiteout
The Lost Treasure of Bogus Bluff
November Gales

www.danbomkamp.com